"Beautifully Flawed"

Demontre ThePoet

Regal Rhythms Poetry LLC
P.O. Box 317746
Cincinnati, Ohio 45231

This book is a work of fiction. Names, characters, places, and incidents are products of the author's imagination, or are used fictitiously. Any resemblance to actual events or locales or persons, living or dead, is entirely coincidental. Library of Congress Cataloging-in-Publication Data is available upon request.

©2023 by Demontre ThePoet

All rights reserved. No part of this book may be reproduced in any form or by any means whatsoever. For more information write Regal Rhythms Poetry LLC.

Cover design: Adam Hayden
Publisher & Editor: Regal Rhythms Poetry LLC

Manufactured in the United States of America
ISBN: 979-8-9879871-2-4
Ebook ISBN: 979-8-9879871-3-1

Dedication

This book is dedicated to my parents, Ronald & Margaret Lewis; my brother, Devrin; & my children, Daunte, Peyton, Raegan & Dawn. I love y'all.

Positive Moves- Moving Forward- The Movement

Follow Me On:

YouTube: Demontre ThePoet Lewis
TikTok: demontrelewis
Facebook: Demontre Lewis (ThePoet)
Facebook: SirRaun Lewis (ThePoet)
Instagram: demontrethepoet

Table of Contents

Dedication 3

Table of Contents 4

Chapter 1: Lewis' Life 6
    Stay (Part 1) 7
    Stay (Part 2) 10
    Stay (Part 3) 13
    Self-Love 17
    My Beautiful Queen 20
    I Am 22
    Lonely Soul, Writing in my Notebook 25
    Evil Power of Money 27
    Why Couldn't You Stay 30
    Guns 32

Chapter 2: SirRaun's Soul 34
    My Notebook Sheets 35
    How True Happiness Is Made 38
    Divorce 41
    The Beauty Within 44
    A Healed Heart 47
    My Dark Abyss 50
    Forever 52
    Truly Missed 55
    Insomnia's Cure 59
    Aggravation 62

Chapter 3: Tre's Thoughts 65
    Come With Me Baby 66
    Washing All the Pain Away 68
    Take a Look 70
    Whenever You Need Me 73
    Hey Ms. Lady 76
    Shattered Pieces 80

Time and Time Again 83

Symptoms of Being in Love 86

My Poisonous Downfall 89

Chapter 4: Montre's Memoirs 92

Working On the Frontline (2020) 93

You Said Goodbye 96

Demons Chasing Me 99

So Many Unanswered Questions 102

Beautifully Black 104

I love LOVE & I hate HATE 107

Her Precious Pearl 110

POETRY is Me 112

Poetry is Me (Part 2) 114

I Grab My Pen 116

Chapter 5: Demontre's Dissertation 118

The Most Beautiful Woman That I've Ever Seen 119

Two Insecure Souls 122

Two Victims DEAD 125

Death 127

A Fair Chance 129

Please Still Love Me 131

Free (Longer Version) 133

A Mind Full of Ideas That's Locked 135

Individuals Divided 138

Many Teardrops 141

Your Only Son 143

Can't Get Things Right 145

The Last Time 147

Never 149

Chapter 1: Lewis' Life

My brother, Devrin & I

Stay (Part 1)

At 11 years old, we went to the same middle school,
How important you would end up to me, I never knew.
You were always so pretty to me,
You'll always be a fancy sight to see.
You grew up to be a classy woman - independent and strong,
The feelings I had for you, I knew couldn't be wrong.
You needed me to express the feelings I had for you,
from time to time,
But I never opened up to you and kept my deepest feelings
about you locked in my mind.
All you wanted was for me to open up to you,
and mean what I say,
But I kept my feelings bottled up,
so I'm not mad that you didn't stay.
I was barely 18 when your dark chocolate complexion
and pearly white smile took my heart.
I never dreamed that I would have to get used
to living my life with us apart.
I couldn't give you the big ceremony
with the horse and carriage,
But it was a happy day for me when we united in marriage.
We started out so full of life,
Although many disagreed –
I was honored that you were my wife.

You started to feel like we shouldn't be together,

I kept forcing our union,

because I thought our union was supposed to last forever.

My other half wasn't happy,

but I didn't listen to what she had to say,

so I'm not mad at all that you didn't stay.

I can't believe how long it's really been,

You were supposed to be off limits,

because you're my cousin's best friend.

We finally started dating and I was floating on air,

I know I kept my feelings distant, but for you I really did care.

I miss waking up and seeing a text from you saying,

"Good morning, Sunshine,"

you were my sexy love,

and lately you've been heavy on my mind.

It's good that we still keep in touch -

you're one of the realist women I've ever known,

but I wish more love between us could've been shown.

You wanted our relationship to blossom,

but I wasn't ready for us to be that way,

So I'm not mad at all that you didn't stay.

We were coworkers when we met

& I was stunned by your pretty face.

I remember being partnered with you

& my heart would always race.

We came from 2 different Worlds,

so I doubt that you noticed me at first.

I was too shy to say anything

& keeping that to myself was the worst.

But suddenly, we grew close-

becoming friends with occasional benefits.

But I did love you, so it didn't matter who you ended up with.

I finally stepped up & was truly happy to be your man,

so I was in total shock

when you no longer wanted to take my hand.

We grew apart, but I was willing to fix it

but you didn't feel the same at the end of the day –

it hurt watching you move on in such a hasty way.

True colors were shown

& that's why I'm not mad that you didn't stay.

My emotions are all over the place

and I'm back to being lonely again,

When it comes to matters of the heart

I simply can't seem to win.

I know my faults and I'm sorry for the times

I may have caused fighting,

So I'm apologizing right now and I'm putting it in writing.

At the end of it all, happiness is my only wish,

Hopefully, one day I can live in complete bliss.

I can't believe how quickly the years have gone away,

A hurt heart is where my emotions lay.

I know love will find me again, so I'll patiently wait for that day,

Then, in love I will be and in love I will stay..........

Stay (Part 2)

Things didn't work out with your mother & I
and your dad wasn't there,
so I was more than happy to take you in as my own.
No matter what happens, just know that with me,
you'll always have a home.
Dawn, I'm excited to have you as MY DAUGHTER
– you were my child before I had one,
I'll always see you as that 2-year-old girl
who was always so full of fun.
The years have gone fast
& it's so hard for any parent to watch their kids grow up,
I miss when times were much simpler for both of us.
The struggle has been real over the years,
but we're making it through,
You're my beautiful baby girl & I'm blessed to have you.
I wish I could give you the world,
but we know that life doesn't ever really work that way,
But whether we're close or far apart
just know my love will always STAY.

I know I'm always hard on you, but I just want you to succeed.
I wouldn't be much of a father, if I didn't push you to be
successful in life & make sure you have all the things you need.
Daunte, "MY SON" - I'm so proud when I say that.
I love that you're in my life & wouldn't take anything that
happened in our past back.

Many times I look at you

& it freaks me out because you're me all over again.

I didn't see it earlier,

but I now know why people say that you're my twin.

The years have brought some hardships,

but we're blessed still in all,

Always stay focused on your goals

& you'll bounce back if you ever fall.

You're my baby boy,

& no matter how old you get it'll always be that way,

No matter where life may take you

know my love is here to STAY.

It was news for me that was Heaven sent,

I still remember the day your Mama said that she was pregnant.

Blessings come when you least expect them to,

I looked forward to raising you,

& spending the rest of my life loving you.

I make it a point to say I love you,

because expression has always been hard for me,

I've learned that saying how you feel in life truly is the key.

Times get so rough and I'm far from perfect

& I know that's not what you expect me to be.

But as long as I'm alive,

I'll strive to make sure you're happy.

My life has been painful

& I just hope that my pain or baggage

may never drive you away.

I just want to say, Peyton, MY LOVE FOR YOU IS

ETERNAL & my love is here to STAY.

I'm saying "Hello" to Raegan, "MY YOUNGEST CHILD,"

I'm patiently waiting for your growth

& times have truly been wild.

I'm loving seeing you get older

& I was proud watching you take your 1st steps,

You speaking your 1st words is something I won't ever forget.

My precious baby girl, I pray you're always healthy & full of life,

Through the hard times your Daddy will be there to help

because life can be such a fight.

I've seen a lot & although I'm still learning,

I'll teach my experiences to you.

My support & love reaches very far

& it'll be there in whatever you do.

All life is golden

& you are yet another of my many blessings,

You're another reminder that life's good

despite all of its stressing.

I'll protect you – I'll love you & I'll be there every day,

Throughout all hurt – the good days & the bad ones please

always know that my love is here to STAY.

Stay (Part 3)

You've always had my back no matter who I am or who I was.
You're my only sibling – MY BROTHER,
we share the same parents and the same blood.
Over the years we've dealt with a lot,
and we have seen many things change,
But I'm glad to know that our loyalty to each other
has always remained the same.
You're an uncle to my children
and I love the way you took on that role,
You're there without a doubt and that's why they love you so.
Through all of life's obstacles
we are brothers and there's nothing that can change that.
I have your back and you have mine
if either one of us is ever under attack.
Nothing can come between us
and the family love
we have is something neither one of us has to say.
But to make things crystal clear
– I am here to say, that the bond we have will always STAY.

I often find it hard to find the exact words
to truly express how I feel about you,
You are the strongest woman I've ever known,
and I work hard to make sure you know this is true.

We've been through it all,

and the fact I still have you in my life

shows that I'm still blessed.

Time as flown by fast

and we've both helped each other

through hardships and much stress.

You are my backbone, and I don't want you to ever forget that,

I love you dear MOTHER OF MINE,

and every kind word I've said about you,

I would never take back.

It was you who pushed me when I wanted to give up,

It was you who helped me out of depression's abyss

when I was trapped and stuck.

I'll love you for always and forever- every year

 – every month – every week and every day,

I cherish your very essence and presence,

– I am always here for you and my love will always STAY.

If I could just spend another day with you

it would be an endless joy that day would bring.

To be able to have your soul risen back to the living

would be such a tremendous thing.

Through my darkest hours,

it's your teachings that helps me and gets me by.

I still strive to make you proud,

and I will continue to try until the day that I die.

I still plan my work then work my plan

exactly the way you taught me.

I've grown & matured a lot

& it saddens me that any further growth

you won't be here to see.

But I know that your soul still exists,

and that can't ever be replaced – killed or destroyed.

Ever since you've been gone,

I've had a certain emptiness - a painful, unfillable void.

My DEAR FATHER,

your hard work and dedication to us all

is remembered and missed every day.

The pain of losing you remains

& though physically gone, I'm glad your influence

& love will always STAY.

I've lived through this journey we all call life

– through the good & bad, I've learned to just pray.

Faith can be a hard thing to have,

but you must never let your faith stray.

Many times, on many days & nights,

a hurtful place has been where my emotions have had to lay.

Doing what you thought was right can get you done wrong,

but you must not let the good within you sway.

Loyalties will be tested – people turn on you

- even ones that you thought would never do you that way.

I've faced all of this & more.

I was left lost & confused,

 – simply speechless without anything to say.

I've seen betrayal many times,

but I survived it

& I'm blessed to still be here to talk about it today.

Deep inside, I am a happy soul,

and nothing will ever break me or take that away.

I am ME, and who I am is strong

– my essence is something that nothing can ever slay.

I am DEMONTRE

& my energy & love is spread

amongst you all & there it will always STAY.

Self-Love

Take all your shattered pieces & put them all back together,
Through all life endeavors
if you're positive then that energy can last forever.
In life it's pretty much a guarantee that you won't always win,
Use the strength you have within to never ever give in.
It's okay if some don't like you for what you say or do,
As long as you push forward and stay true to you.
It is impossible to love someone or anything else,
If you're not at first in love with yourself.
Always have Self-Love.

I learned many years ago,
that pain & love will always go hand & hand.
Stay strong through all that's wrong
& keep spreading love as much as you can.
Constantly push forward,
because progress won't be made moving backwards at all.
Make positive moves through the negative times
& make sure you get up anytime you may fall.
A Strength Within is what resides inside us,
so tap into that potential and you'll go far.
Be the Rose that grew from concrete
 - Be the last one standing - be a shining star.

They can't break the unbreakable,

so always be that impenetrable, boulder rock,

No matter if they scheme & plot,

be determined to be a MOVEMENT

that can't be stopped.

Always have Self-Love.

You can smile, but you'll still know tears.

But always be thankful for every breath.

You can be brave, but you'll still know fears,

but still living means you don't know death.

You'll know order, just like you'll know chaos

- you'll know victory, just like you'll know loss.

There's strength mixed in tears,

you may cry, so don't ever give up at any cost.

When you feel stuck

& don't know what your next move in life should be.

When those demons from the past come

& have you questioning if your soul will ever feel free.

Remember your losses can be victories,

if you learn from them & still succeed.

Keep pushing forward,

because we all have people that depend on us

& we all got kids to feed.

Always have Self-Love.

Lately, I've been sitting at home, all alone

just trying to heal from all of my life's pain.

But I don't want you to feel sorry for me,

because I know many are going through the same.

Self-Love is what you must achieve,

because with it you'll have a calm feeling enter your brain.

When you're on the brink of feeling insane,

Self-Love will heal you & once again make you sane.

I was a suicidal alcoholic,

but I'm still here.

- I'm literally living proof that it's nothing to fear.

You can & will make it throughout all these hard

- painful - and trying years.

Just never give in - trust me,

when I say that in the end - you will eventually win.

Just always practice Self-Love,

and connect with the strength that we all have within.

Always have Self-Love.

My Beautiful Queen

You keep me dry in a storm,

When it snows your love keeps me warm.

My father's death was our greatest pain,

But your strength helps me to maintain.

You made me believe,

You give me everything that I need.

Life's been such a hard fight,

One day, we'll finally see the light.

You are an angel that came down,

You helped me turn my life around.

Everyone in this world knows,

Friends will come and friends will go.

Even though we don't agree sometimes,

Your love frees my mind.

Even though we don't always see eye to eye,

I'll always be by your side.

With you behind me, I can always win,

I will have a victory no matter what battle I am in.

Through it all, you are always there,

It's the same hurt and joy that we share.

I'm always going to be near,

I swear you will have nothing to fear.

I am forever here,

I will make your rainy days clear.

I will take away every dark cloud,

My love for you will never be in doubt.

I remember every holiday,

I remember all the loving things that you had to say.

I remember when Granddaddy died,

We both held each other and cried.

I remember all the good times that the hard times can't erase,

I pray that your heart stays in a happy and peaceful place.

Every day and every night I pray,

That your sweet and caring love never goes away.

Wow - I need you so much I never knew,

That I just can't see my life without you.

You're always there for me when I'm stressed,

You pick me up when I am depressed.

Your love is so true,

I can't say it enough - I need you.

Every day I work hard to be the man I'm supposed to be,

I will not stop until I know you're proud of me.

No matter how far apart - in my heart, we are always together,

You're my backbone - I'll love you forever.

You are a blessing for me, my children, and my brother.

This is for my beautiful Queen - my mother.

I Am

I am the reason that you cried yourself to sleep
from a broken heart that night,
I am the reason you love when they hug & hold you tight.
I am the reason you're bitter & do mean things out of spite,
I am the reason it hurts so bad when y'all argue & fight.
I am the reason you stayed when you weren't appreciated,
I am the reason bitter feelings of regret have been created.

I am the reason you won't let the past go,
I am the reason it's hard for you
to ever again let your emotions show.
I am the reason the pain in your heart
has invisible permanent scars,
I am the reason you let hateful feelings
allow you to take matters way too far.
I am the reason why emotional pain is such a nightmare,
I am the reason you hold hope that they still might care.

I am the reason you're scared to hold anyone close,
I am the reason betrayal hurts the most.
I am the reason you wish happy days
together would've lasted forever,
I am the reason you wish that y'all could've ended it better.
I am the reason when y'all fell out, it felt like a living hell,
I am fake, but I am also real and most times it's hard to tell.

I am the reason you should move on,

but you still keep in touch,

I am most often confused with lust.

I am the reason you stayed after you clearly had enough,

I am the reason you stayed when things were rough & tough.

I am the reason when you should've left, but you still fought,

I am the reason that you didn't let that horrible relationship

simply be an afterthought.

I am a different experience for everyone

- the stories about me are never the same,

I am colder than ice - I am hotter than a flame

& I am way more hurt than any pain.

The loss of me can & will drive a sane person insane.

People seek me out, because I soothe their heart

& bring peace to their brain,

They yearn for me, even though I am known

to make an endless pain on them rain,

I cause much aggravation, but my presence remains the same.

I am the reason you tried so hard to make it work,

I am the reason you can't take it when your heart hurts.

I am intoxicating

- the need of what I am is what people can't get rid of,

I am addictive like drugs & I'm what everyone has dreamed of.

I am everything that these words have said I was,

I am hurt; I am joy; I am true; I AM……. LOVE.

Lonely Soul, Writing in my Notebook

I'm just a lonely soul. writing in my notebook,
if you're not too busy you can come take a look.

I got many thoughts that's in my mind,
I'm writing them all down to pass the time.
I wonder, will I get murdered or die of natural causes,
In the game of life, I've had many losses.
Will I go to hell & fry,
or will I pass on & live in the sky?

When our body is lifeless, where does our soul really go,
Why is it so hard to tell friends from foes?
Too many people sit back & judge me,
even the ones who claim they love me.

I'm desperately trying to show a perspective
from my point of view so come take a look,
Please see the thoughts of a lonely soul,
writing in my notebook.

I'm a good person, but I'm not treated that way,
People claim they love me, but only got negative stuff to say.
I've got a good heart, but I've done some bad,
& it's sad when I think about all the drama my life has had.

For that very reason, I stay to myself,

People will use your weakness against you

- that's why I hate accepting help.

I'm staying out of sight & not bothering anyone,

I'm going to just do me & raise my daughter & son.

I'm staying away from everyone & I think that's best,

I'm writing this to get all this off my chest.

If you're not too busy,

you can flip through my pages

and take a look,

I'm just a lonely soul, writing in my notebook.

Evil Power of Money

Many people think having tons of cash is best,

but I've seen it bring nothing but a lot of stress,

I try hard not to be a slave to it,

but I can't do without it - that's something I must confess.

Not having it can bring unhappy times

- but having it doesn't always bring peace to your mind,

When you finally get it, some problems are cured,

but it brings more - so you're stuck in its grind.

We're in a world of evil & money is the root.

- People will kill for it - we all know that's the truth,

Although I know this all too well, I still go out every day

to earn it, because I gotta feed my youth.

But there's still many things money can't buy

- like self-respect or self-pride,

Money can't give you a sunset or sunrise

& you can't take it with you when you die.

But even with that well known fact,

I still signed up for overtime cause I can't live without it,

I get insecure when my account gets low

& the little self-confidence I do have I start to doubt it.

You can work so hard & not have a lot afterwards to show

- It's sad how our world goes,

You can't break this cycle anytime soon,

because over everything money has control.

Money controls our whole Nation

& you even need it to obtain a higher education.

It improves many situations,

but all the while it creates a debt that can last for generations.

It'll cause death and lots of tears

& it'll make families fall out and not talk for years,

No matter the issues it causes it'll always be here

& no matter what we all will keep it near.

It'll continue to bring violence on our streets

& continue to cause no mercy for the weak,

It gives power to those who shouldn't have power

& give clout to their voices when they speak.

Greed & money destroys the simple things

& makes demons out of decent human beings,

It brings a cloud of selfishness

& just to get to it people will take unnecessary means.

It'll give a good person a dark heart

- behind every robbery, money plays the motivating part,

I miss my times as a kid before the strain

& pain that the need of money would eventually start.

I'm utterly exhausted,

but I signed up again for overtime

cause 40 hours a week ain't enough.

I deal with long days that are rough,

because without more money these bills make things tough.

A clear state of mind & a well-rested body,

sadly, isn't my priority right now - I'm trying to make it,

So, I push everything aside because I'm earning my keep out

here instead of trying to take it.

As I hustle to pay the rent

- I sit & start to wonder where all of the good times have went,

But I realize that the good times die abruptly

once all of the money gets spent.

I swear - I work up such a sweat

to barely have a decent check - it's something I truly regret,

Because I bet once those taxes hit,

I won't get nearly the amount that I expect.

Because it's just like what my parents would always say

 - on any given night or day,

It goes faster than you make it,

so you better have some stock or savings

& put some of it away.

Money talks and the rest walks

& that's how it'll be until we're all outlined in chalk,

You can't make it without it, so please don't come at me with

that "moncy isn't everything" talk.

But at the same time, it's not the solver of all problems

which is the sad song we all sing,

and for the false security it brings,

it seems many are willing to do anything.

It is very tragic - sad & nowhere near funny,

Our whole world is run by the evil power of money.

Why Couldn't You Stay

I miss the old Demontre,
So, I'm going to write to him today.
I'm writing this piece to my old self,
I'm not trying to scare him - I just want to help.

Demontre - we're so insecure now,
I don't know what to say.
I miss the days we were just kids and all we did was just play.
I wish the love in your heart can stay with you,
I wish the kids that we have now could go back in time
and play with you.

I know you're happy and full of life,
But, sadly, our future isn't so bright.
There is a lot of pain ahead,
some of our joy will be stress instead.

You're going to fight
with those you consider family and friends,
and sometimes it seems that sad days will never end.
Hard times are going to hurt your soul,
and when will hard times end, nobody knows.

Our Daddy's gone and it hurts so bad.

His suicide is going to leave you depressed and sad.

You're going to lose Eugene

- Aunt Debby, plus Grandma Lewis

and Granddaddy James too.

So, please appreciate the time that they spend with you.

We're going to have kids and they are so adorable,

They will give you hope in a world that is horrible.

College didn't quite work out, but there's still time to go back,

Please stay focused on our goals, so our life can stay on track.

Looking back at times we were so naive,

a lot of our dreams won't come true

and at times, it'll be hard to still believe.

Demontre - I really do miss the way we were,

I think that's the reason we are always staying buzzed.

I hate the fact that it's hard to stay sober,

I wish I could start everything over.

My old self has gone completely away,

Oh Lord, why couldn't he stay?????????????

Guns

GUNS - many people hate them,
because they have way too much power,
they're fatal at any given minute or hour.
People carelessly use them not knowing the cost,
it's their fault that so many lives have been lost.

GUNS - people mistakenly used them at will,
their only purpose is to injure and kill.
They cause agony and make loved ones cry,
their presence has caused so many to die.

GUNS - their presence changes the good into evil,
but people bring them around
knowing the grief they can bring to people.
They violently bring people to their end,
and they aid in making our world full of sin.

GUNS - because of them many are dead and gone,
they are used irresponsibly & makes right situations go wrong.
They can cause riots between whole crowds, and sadly,
they have murdered somebody's child.

GUNS - they leave bodies lifeless and cold,
hearing and reading about their deadly stories
have gotten so old.
When they pop off,
it leaves people in a complete and permanent silence,
they are the reason a simple argument
can be blown out of proportion and end in violence.

GUNS - they spread misery and so much pain,
but we keep using them, so mankind is the one to blame.
When they come out people end up in a coffin,
they are the reason we attend funerals so often.

GUNS - they take away the good
- the bad - the old and the young,
When they are used - death is what tends to come.
They have tragically made so many heartbeats stop,
every time they let off their deadly shots.

We have lost fathers - mothers - daughters and sons,
and that's the reason we should all hate them
- please put down the GUNS.

Chapter 2: SirRaun's Soul

My oldest daughter, Dawn & I

My Notebook Sheets

On my Notebook sheets

- I express how much I'm thankful to be alive,

Because these days there's too much happiness that's a lie.

On nights that I get restless & I'm tossing & turning in my bed,

Thinking of all the pressure that's on me to keep my family fed.

I turn to my Notebook sheets

and my pen puts that stress to rest,

It pushes away negative vibes

– helping the positive ones stay & that's what's best.

When I know it's something missing and I'm feeling incomplete,

I grab my pen and release my thoughts

– ridding myself of any pain on my Notebook sheets.

I'm a stand-up man and I take care of all my responsibilities,

and I work hard to be a good father to the best of my abilities.

Walking the straight path can be so hard at times

- I'm just out here trying to do what's right,

making it through all of life's struggles and fights.

When I'm on the brink of insanity, I write

& put my soul into my pen.

Filling up my Notebook sheets,

writing whatever comes to mind to bring peace to myself again.

My dear Grandma & my father to are both transitioned
into eternal peace above,
I keep faith in the hope that I'll see them again
when I transcend & be reunited with their love.

I plan my work, then I work my plan
in the same way my father would preach,
I always push forward
although at times it feels
that I'm working toward goals that's out of reach.
Most of my dreams are nightmares
and they all seem to somehow come true.
I'm terrified
& I don't want to suffer any longer,
so retreating to my Notebook sheets is what I do.
As a child, I didn't have much to say
- all I did was run around & play all night and day,
But now that I've grown to a man
all that carefree lifestyle has gone away.
I miss the innocence that was carried inside
and out of me when I was a child,
I still carry the same passion for happiness
as my life has slowly gone from mild to wild.
This is not all being said, so that you can feel sorrow for me,
I'm once again turning negative to positive
by turning to my Notebook sheets as you can see.
I'm transforming the hurt that's witnessed
when you look into my eyes,

And turning it into hope

because no matter what I must continue to rise.

Not sure if I'll make it to be elderly or pass tomorrow,

because life's an unpredictable game,

So, I leave my legacy on my Notebook sheets speaking for

those who didn't get a chance to & that's such a shame.

I used to use gallons of liquor poured into my cup

to drown out my pain,

But that's no longer needed

for my Notebook sheets is all I need to keep me sane.

I'm in love with my first love which is my Notebook sheets,

so I wrote this piece to explain why.

My affection for them will never die

- over the years it only multiplies.

So whenever something's missing,

on pain filled nights that I once again feel incomplete,

I start writing again, spilling out all emotions

good or bad

on my Notebook sheets.

How True Happiness Is Made

I fell for you when I was barely grown & it was way too soon.
You brought me so much joy
that I never thought you could be my doom.
You made me so carefree & brought me out of my shy cocoon,
At any party or club, you always brought life into the room.
The happy illusion you gave me- false, but I fell in love,
I swear you had me in a trance - you're my favorite drug.
I needed you
- your presence was something I just couldn't get rid of,
You falsely supported me while others sat back & judged.
You were never far from me & I always stayed close to you,
In many ways, you were my crutch in everything
that I used to do.
I stayed with you even though you brought me many blues,
You were the cause of so much of my ridicule.
People began to hate when I brought you around,
but I ignored what they had to say,
We were a package deal,
so they had to just except us in this way.
People would argue with me about you,
but I told them you were here to stay.
Nobody took me seriously about you,
because you did bring stressful days.

They just didn't understand,

because they never felt the feelings you gave to me.

They never did understand

the many nights that you actually made me happy.

But in the end, they were right in thinking

our relationship should never be,

They saw it many years ago & now I finally see.

You were my support - you held me down,

But you were killing me in the process,

so I decided to turn my life around.

You were unhealthy for me

- you made my body ache & my head pound.

So many times you'd have me paranoid

- a peace of mind with you was something I never found.

You were someone to relate to me when I was stressed,

You were a quick fix on hard nights

when I was feeling depressed.

I became addicted to you - or should I say obsessed,

I needed your companionship

- you helped me on days of unrest.

But sadly, your help wasn't real help

- you covered up the pain and didn't heal it.

You were a short-term bandage

- as far as my stress, you never killed it.

My depression always stayed

- every time you left, I would still feel it.

You weren't a good fit for me

- dealing with my issues without you ended up being the real fit.

You were my longest relationship

even though most of my time spent with you I can't even recall,

Me being loyal to only you, almost caused my own downfall.

I pushed away so many for you,

because I didn't know how to ignore you when you would call,

But I've finally broken free of my addiction to ALCOHOL.

I'm done with the drunken nights

that caused me much embarrassment.

I look at all the time I wasted with you

& wonder where all that time went.

No more blacking out

& not remembering what happened the night before,

No more taking my last dollars

& cents & spending them at the liquor store.

In the mirror, I now see a much healthier guy,

you look at me & you can see the relief in each of my eyes.

It's very clear now when you take a look into my face,

That I'm doing well now

- I'm in a happier place.

I took off my shackles & I'm no longer an alcoholic slave,

Through my now sober eyes, I see how true happiness is made.

Divorce

It's because happy days had been gone too long
is how this came to be,
Peace of mind could no longer be found at home,
so I'm relieved the end came for me.
It started out with us saying we would be always and forever,
but now it would be too soon,
if I saw her never again….. EVER.

She never deserved the honor of being given
a man's family last name,
I was warned, but I was too young
& dumb to see that I was heading into pain.
It should've been my happily ever after
but it turned into a war I couldn't win,
It should've been a dream come true
but it turned into a nightmare that finally came to an end.
I reminisce on days & nights, I was left speechless & frustrated
& having nothing to say.
I reminisce on how 360 things went,
as all the love slowly faded away.
The torture of trying to force a dying love that was rotted out
- expired and old,
Having a hate grow inside of me
because I showed unconditional love but got treated cold.

Long gone are the days

when what had taken place was our 1st kiss,

All the fighting & heartache - getting played & cheated on

- I'll never miss.

I was haunted by a bad decision

- that had me livin' & sleeping with the enemy.

At the time, I couldn't see that I was holding onto nothing

but misery.

I love her daughter as my own, plus we had a son

& for them to witness this is unfair,

But I had to fight & care for my own happiness

& for the 1st time in my life peace is there.

The shame I felt for playing a fool's role

was enough to drive any man insane,

I stop caring who's at fault

- I'm done with the finger pointing & playing the blame game.

Many years passed & the bitterness on her side stays present,

but it won't be my downfall,

Because truth be told - her cheating ways

& thirst to see greener grass is what ended us after all.

Then when it wasn't better on the other side,

she wanted me to amend things, but it was too late.

I learned after many times being burned that trying to rekindle

things would be a mistake.

To stay relevant, social media is used to slander me

but I refuse to be a partner in that dance,

Trying to bait me into fighting & interrupt my newfound peace

but I won't give her that chance.

You can't have a clear mind

when you're in drama & confusion, so it was best to stay away,

Once you know your self-worth,

what the negative ones may say will never ruin your days.

Our past teaches, so I don't get mad

when old pictures are seen showing a once happy time.

Those are just chapters that ended

& new chapters started keeps happiness in my mind.

Being able to move on while watching my kids grow

is what brought peace to my heart,

I'm glad to let the anger go,

because it certainly would have ripped me completely apart.

I'm proof that happiness comes better late than never,

so remember, it doesn't have to be forced.

For my life truly began……. After my Divorce.

The Beauty Within

It's the beauty within that makes your smile so grand,
It makes me feel so lucky that you took my hand.
It's the beauty within that makes our relationship
such a blessing,
It helps me pass the hardships that life uses when it's testing.
It's the beauty within that makes our love for each other
a success,
It's truly the reason that you are the best.
It's the beauty within that makes me love
that twinkle in your eye,
It lets me know that no matter what, we will always get by.
It's the beauty within that makes our bond so strong,
It makes our life play out like a wonderful melody,
in a beautifully played song.
It's the beauty within that heals each other's pain.
Fate brought us together,
and things for the better have changed.

It's the beauty within that leaves me speechless
every time you come in my presence,
You remind me how lovely love is in its purest essence.
It's the beauty within that makes our connection
such a passionate ride,
It makes our home a happy one
no matter where we may reside.

It's the beauty within that makes me happy

whenever I hold you in my arms,

We keep each other stable & push away what may cause harm.

It's the beauty within that makes my life impossible

without you,

Every good thought I've ever had

- has been about you.

It's the beauty within that makes me miss you so much

when I'm away,

I need you every day & my affection for you will always stay.

It's the beauty within that gives our love it's spark

& me a happy heart,

It's literally a work of art - I've loved you from the start.

It's the beauty within that makes you my Angel

in this world of sin,

It was joyful the way our love got to begin & it'll never end.

It's the beauty within that makes my feelings sing,

It's such a wonderful thing

- I want the world to know what it means.

It's the beauty within that completes my soul.

On the inside I glow - I'm in love with the way our love flows.

It's the beauty within that takes me to a new high,

With you by my side, I feel as if I can fly.

It's the beauty within which makes you

the one I adore,

I want & need you more & more

- you healed my heart which once was sore.

It's the beauty within you

that completes the beauty that is within me,

With you, I feel alive and free

- I'm blessed our love is here to be.

I love that love has found me again,

With you, I'll always win

- I'll forever love you inside & out,

- but it starts with THE BEAUTY WITHIN.

A Healed Heart

It's probably because subconsciously,
there's a fear of being lonely.
But the love that was displayed was far from being phony.
Many of us have issues letting go,
because of the pain that comes from moving on,
The anguish of letting someone you care for be gone.
Those memories stay, but they're no longer around,
You had high hopes, but in the end, you got let down.
Two hearts hurt in a breakup,
so don't harp on who's wrong or right.
Because you should focus on the fact
that y'all no longer have to fight.
No amount of love is worth having grudges
and holding on to blame,
Don't let your once calm
& cool emotions become heated - irritated & inflamed.

Everyone knows how negative a relationship ending
can change someone,
so being positive is the key when a bad ending may come.
Let bitterness be a thing of the past,
The pain of breaking up hurts,
but that pain will never forever last.
It just means that a new chapter is upon you,
A chance for you to start over brand new.

You may be stressed and depressed at the same time.
But in times of unrest you're still blessed,
so you must see the signs.
It's your moment to just let things go,
It's your moment to just let new things
come into your life and flow.

There will be times that doubt will still creep
into your mind state,
And they'll still be times that you'll feel
as if loneliness will forever be your fate.
Love is an everlasting emotion,
so don't expect to completely lose the feeling.
Your emotions will go back and forth,
but that's just the natural process while you're still healing.
Hearts never break evenly, so don't compare your pain
with another person's sorrow,
Take things day by day,
and just know that with the future
comes a better tomorrow.
Hold on & stay strong and remember better days,
Take time to free your mind
& just accept the fact that your life is now in a new phase.
A new journey is scary, but it's normal to feel uneasy,
And it's going to take a while before you're comfortable,
with a new journey completely.

Embrace the fact that love lost is a chance
for a new love to be gained,
Embrace the truth that you will eventually heal from all pain.
Embrace the sunny days that will come after this stormy rain,
Embrace the faith that you had in love,
because the suffering it may have caused, didn't happen in vain.
We've all been burned, but it's just lessons we all had to learn,
Nobody deserves a hurt heart,
but sadly, with that we've all had our turn.
Have patience
- your time of healing has already begun to start.
You are stronger than you know,
so breakups will never rip you apart.
Your future will be incredible
- your moment is now, so make sure you play your part.
Even though it takes time,
happiness shines all around you,
Please embrace it once you have a HEALED HEART.

My Dark Abyss

Things are so rough these days,

My innocent days seem so far away.

I often wonder what happened to the way things used to be,

But missing things from my past is an everyday thing for me.

I always knew life wouldn't be completely fair,

But I'm shocked at how so many people

out there simply don't care.

My hard times was cutting me really deep,

But I was able to climb up my mountain of trials

in life even though it was very steep.

I had fell flat not too long ago - I was a broken man,

I couldn't get things right, so I left it in God's hands.

I had to man up & swallow my pride,

I had to continue to live life, although on the inside I had died.

I stayed strong & I eventually saw the light,

I'm in a good place now because I continued to fight.

My son & daughters were my motivation

I just couldn't let them down.

Even when times seemed awful,

I know their love is still around.

I knew at the end of it all

the answer to my problems started with me,

I made a choice not to sit back & just let the dark times be.

Life is truly what you make it, most of the time,

That's why during any of my negative times,

I try hard to keep a positive state of mind.

Deep in my heart, I knew happy days were ahead,

So, I didn't focus on the bad, I focused on the good instead.

I stopped trying to be who I thought people wanted me to be,

And I learned to just spread love, so now I live life happily.

I was mopping floors & cleaning bathrooms

just to make ends meet,

And I love my family & friends for not giving up on me

when times got really bleak.

You accepted me with my flaws & all,

I've got nothing but love for all of y'all.

Over the years, plenty of tears have been shed

over lost loved ones that we all still hold dear.

Death is a promise that's always kept

- so, we must be thankful for the days that we're still here.

Though it's very painful,

that my Father is no longer among the living

I know he's an Angel watching over me now,

When life has treated me foul,

vivid memories of him make me smile.

I learned that I have to make my own destiny,

I had a moment of truth

& it was a beautiful sight for me to see.

I had to sit back & reminisce,

about all the good times that I truly miss.

Life had me down & I didn't know this much pain could exist.

I stayed strong & God granted my wish,

Happiness came back in my life

- I made it out of my Dark Abyss.

Forever

Your words are simply wonderful - beautiful & so divine,
I'm in love with your very presence - you blow people's minds.
I'm far from perfect & betrayal is the worst thing
that can be seen,
I'll always work to give you my everything.
No matter how bad the weather,
my love and appreciation of you is FOREVER.
I honestly don't trust anyone else.
So, it helps that I can write you,
my love for what you represent is beyond true.
You'll never be silenced,
because you've got an unforgettable thunderous voice,
There's no doubt, that in life
you'll always be my one and only choice.
Beautiful is what you are,
I've loved you for years from afar.
I was barely 12 years old,
when I fell in love with you, and I've loved you ever since.
I should've embraced you so much sooner,
but I just didn't have the confidence.
Through the uninspired times dealing with writer's block,
I pray you'll always help me express what I need to say.
My heart is with you
and that's where it's going to FOREVER stay.

Our connection is love in its purest form.

You soothe my agony & brought calm,

when the anger inside of me had started to storm.

At times when I wanted to give up

- my counseling through you, gave me the strength to still fight.

The sheer beauty of you is what inspires me

to continue to write.

You've always been my shoulder,

when I had to deal with life's burdens & pains.

I've changed so much over the years,

but you'll FOREVER remain consistently the same.

With you, I'm always on a natural high,

With you, my soul will always be able to fly.

I've had many people turn on me,

I've gotten blindsided throughout life,

but your beauty is something I always see.

You were there through every funeral and painful death,

You were there during the happy times

and brought out of me the very best.

You traveled with me a lot through the years

giving me a poetic mind state.

My thoughts flow freely,

because becoming one with you has been my fate.

I'm a Poet - an artist because you gave me the gift to express,

I'm lyrically bound to you FOREVER,

because you cured me from when I was hopelessly depressed.

My words through you are heartfelt, even though at times,

people don't see or understand my vision.

My thoughts through you can hit hard,

but are a peaceful collision.

Fictional stories are told

through you, as well as real life endeavors.

I'm in love with your essence,

because you make everything better.

You've stood the test of time, even though life is as

unpredictable as the weather.

This is yet another tribute to the art of Poetry

- and my love for it will be FOREVER.

Truly Missed

It's been so hard to imagine

trying to continue on

without all of you,

But sadly & regretfully

- through it all life will always continue.

I miss my Father and his teachings

which guided me to live my life right,

"Ronny," when my world turns dark & cloud filled,

you become my light & my sight.

My Granddaddy Rev. James inspired me,

every time I went to his church & he would preach.

Although you're gone - through your sermons

- your words are still here to teach.

Cousin Eugene, you not being here still leaves my heart empty

& I don't know what to do,

We all even call my son "Mann"

- he's got the same nickname as you.

I'm hurt by your son being killed

- rest peacefully Jalyn - a victim of guns.

I'm full of much guilt,

for not spending more time with him

 - gone way too young.

Chris, it was a beyond painful moment

when the news got to me that you had died,

I wish I could've seen both yours & my father's pain,

because I could've talked y'all out of suicide.

I've lost 3 Grandmas in my lifetime

& I pray that they have found peace in the clouds above,

Grand Rell - Grandma Lewis & Grandma Johnnie

just always know that I still feel your love.

Aunt Debbie, your passing cut deeply

- I can't explain how I miss you so much.

I desperately wish I could still see you

- hug on you and feel your loving touch.

Cousin Veronica, your endless energy is forever here

& you'll always be our sunshine.

The joy you spread is lasting for an eternity

& is always remembered time after time.

Ms. Vicky, I still hear your infectious laugh,

it plays over & over in my head like an uplifting song.

I hope that your soul will continue to fly,

you're missed & it's hard to believe you're gone.

Ms. Verdell, I still appreciate your guidance

and the way you took me under your wing.

Your pain is now no more

& your spirit is felt every time the birds sing.

My dear Aunt Barbara is eternally resting

on the other side and there isn't any more pain.

I miss seeing you,

but just know, that all the suffering wasn't in vain.

Uncle Larry & my big Cousin - my brother – Larry,
without y'all it's been harder,
I fight so very hard not to allow my heart
to fall into a place that's darker.

Rest Easy Jay and please save a place for me up there,
we'll see each other again one day,
It seems when things are going to be okay
- fate comes and takes another good person away.
To my lil cousin Chester,
- I wish we had more time together.
Cause we didn't get to hang much,
looking at old pics just isn't enough
for your sudden passing, for us all was tough.
Cousin Josh… I never dreamed I would be saying I miss you.
You were taken away unfairly
& the pain that was created is unbearable too.
So many have left me over the years,
but I know in some shape or form they're all still here.
Guiding me through life's pain & tears - ups & downs
- and all of my fears.
When I'm trying to discover life's meaning
or just dealing with stress filled days that come,
It's the memories that we share that turns the bad
into good & I think of times of fun.

I need you all now just like I needed you all back then,
I can't wait until I have the chance to see you all again.
I hope that all your souls are blessed, although physically gone,
that part of you will always exist,
Loving memories of you all inspired me to write this
- for you all are truly missed.

Insomnia's Cure

Restless nights can be the worse,

Many nights my heart races

& in the morning my exhaustion hurts.

Insomnia is my evil & damning curse,

It visits me often & peaceful nights never come first.

I toss & turn, but sleep doesn't come,

I'm so very tired, so where does this restlessness come from?

I yearn for my body to just go numb,

My thoughts can't calm down, because my mind always runs.

My eyes are heavy, but relaxation is what I never see,

I lay in bed, hopelessly awake, sleep is never easy for me.

My mind has cluttered thoughts & I can't set them free,

I try to calm my soul, but I'm forever on this sleepless spree.

I feel tortured - a good night's rest is what my soul needs,

My body drags daily, but when nightfall happens,

trying to get rest is something I can't succeed.

I need rest, but I can't seem to sleep when I lay my head,

It feels like a tug of war between being unconscious,

or conscious in my bed.

Every day goes fast, but the nights just drag along,

Nights of me being well rested seem to always end up wrong.

I break out in cold sweats.

I stay so uncomfortable,

that's why rest filled nights have not found me yet.

Every time I toss & turn more & more,

Each night, I painfully wonder

what that night may have in store.

Every night I'm so wide eyed & awake,

For some reason, once again, insomnia is my fate.

I lay in the dark with my eyes wide open,

Wishing that my sleeping habits wasn't so broken.

I wish in some way drowsiness can finally be found,

I desperately wish for sleep that is sound.

I honestly wish for a deep coma like rest,

To make up for the nights

I sat dealing with huge amounts of stress.

I feel so cursed - I need sleep and rest right now,

I need to lie down and be calm - but I don't know how.

I've missed so much rest over these past few years,

Some of my life shortcomings have caused me tears.

I sit up worrying about countless fears,

I simply dread thinking

about how quickly my end could be near.

I stress over things I can't even control,

How to relieve my mental agony is something I don't know.

Past failures and pain stay with me vividly,

Dreams that never came to be bother me.

I constantly feel like a failure, because of my many losses,

Depression from lost time spent

is sadly one of my sleepiness' causes.

I want to close my eyes, but they stay open wide,

I need to let go of my nervousness

and just let those negative thoughts die.

I've made it through hell and back

- and I've got the scars to show.

I'm still struggling to let those hellish experiences go.

This insomnia is devilishly attacking my everyday pleasure,

It actually has me doubting that every day

I draw breath is a treasure.

But even though I'm clearly a tortured insomniac,

my heart will always stay pure.

I'll sit back and calmly lay here

- until I am able to one day discover INSOMNIA'S CURE.....

Aggravation

Aggravation is giving all you got, but it's not recognized.
It's a painful frustration that can make tears flood your eyes.
Aggravation is that time when you just need one chance,
but you're held back
when you're giving your all to just advance.
Aggravation is your hard work being taken for granted,
Your hopes crumble
& go the opposite way that you had planned it.
Aggravation is when you show love, but it's not appreciated,
It's when everything goes wrong,
but it's not how things were supposed to be slated.
Aggravation is trying to make it in a cold & unforgiving world.
It's not being able to shine through
you're one of life's beautiful pearls.
Aggravation is everything going wrong all at the same time.
It's that overwhelming feeling
when stress takes control of your mind.
Aggravation is when your time is now,
but you're forced to wait,
It's such a damning fate
& it can make a heart full of love fall into hate.
Aggravation is the beautiful struggles of single parenthood
& far too many know exactly what I mean.
Your sacrifices cut deep & more often than not - go unseen.

Aggravation is unanswered love
when you've given someone your heart.
They were supposed to have a starring role in your life,
but they didn't play the part.
Aggravation is the lost feeling people have when life shatters
happiness that you had in store.
Hope had been taken
when you only needed just a little bit more.
Aggravation is a marriage ending,
or losing a relationship that was long term.
You gave it your everything,
but in the end your bond didn't stay firm.
Aggravation is the lonesome feeling that you have when you
miss those who death called away.
You wish you had them back for at least another day
- you have so much more that you wanted to say.
Aggravation is the many times you are misunderstood,
Things are taken badly,
when your intentions were only to spread good.
Aggravation is not being able to express the feelings
that you've got,
Misconceptions take over and leave you lost in your life's plot.
Aggravation is what has you fighting
an unhealthy type of addiction or crave.
You try hard to behave & yearn to not be that addiction's slave.

Aggravation is not being able to live up to high expectations,
You value people's opinion,
but they have no idea the pain that you're always facing.
Aggravation is always being trapped in society's grip
when you just want to be free.
It's so hard to clearly see
- when an insane pain won't let you be.
Aggravation is when you want to scream and yell,
but it won't be much help,
In the end, you must keep control
or run the risk of losing one's self.
Aggravation is a way of life that we all must learn to tackle.
Because no matter what,
- aggravation is always going to be one of many
of our shackles.

Chapter 3: Tre's Thoughts

My only son, Daunte & I

Come With Me Baby

Let's just let our chemistry flow,
girl just let your emotions go
- our connection is strong, we both already know.
I'm curious to feel your kiss,
a night together would be rich
- girl stop trying to resist.
Quit spending your nights alone,
our passion can't be wrong,
- girl come on over to my home.

Give in to our passions and desires,
I feel our heat burning like fire
- it makes my want for you more dire.
We'll put on repeat our favorite slow track.
I'll rub your face while arching your back
- the lights are off, it's better when the room is pitch black.
Just wrap your legs around my face,
let me get a taste of what's in between your waist.

I want to kiss all on your skin.
I'll rub on you softly as I put it in
- then our sweet bliss can begin.
We'll use each other's bodies for pleasure
- we don't need to rush there's no pressure,
it's our fair exchange that we both will treasure.

Let me in between your thighs

- our thirst for each other can't be denied,

as I push in deeper, you'll clinch up and sigh.

We'll grind together & sweat.

We'll reach our peak, but won't stop yet

- I've wanted you badly ever since we first met.

I'm going to do you until you shake

- it's raw passion that we're going to make.

In the morning, our bodies will be both satisfied as well as ache.

Our connection will be very tight

- I want you to myself all night,

come with me babe, don't try to fight.

I promise you'll love this sensation.

Pure ecstasy is what we'll be making

- you'll moan and breathe hard, there will be no faking.

We'll change each other's world

- I'll make your toes curl, let me inside your precious pearl.

I'll have you digging your nails in me - just wait and see,

holding each other close makes us both happy.

Together we'll make erotic sounds.

I'm going to make your juices rain down

- our passion will know no bound.

The connection we have is crazy

- I want you bad, you're such a fine lady,

please take my hand and come with me baby.....

Washing All the Pain Away

They cleanse everything, I wish they could always stay.
Beautiful rain drops - beautiful rain drops,
washing all the pain away.
The rain washes away life's many sins,
It's the rain that calms the many bad moods I'm often in.
The rain soothes the pain and stops the hurt souls from crying,
The rain soothes the pain caused from lost souls
that had been dying.
The rain washes away all pain
and raises my once buried soul & keeps it flying,
Nothing else is the same as the cleansing rain
- there's no denying.
The scent of the beautiful rain
flows through the air and is so refreshing,
The relief the rain brings is such a wonderful blessing.
Staring out my window, I see the rain drops fall,
These rainy days make my mind wonder towards a happy place,
that on any other day, I wouldn't be able to recall.

They cleanse everything, I wish they could always stay.
Beautiful rain drops - beautiful rain drops,
washing all the pain away.
I've soul searched for a long time,
but I still haven't completely found my essence,
But the new life that rain brings is one of many

of nature's presents.

The sound of rain falling down is a beauty no one can question,

It brings such a peaceful mindset and that is such a blessing.

When my Daddy passed away, it rained so hard the day after.

The rain kept my pain calm as my life

reluctantly got sent into a new chapter.

The clear blue sky turns cloudy, but it's still a wonderful sight,

The pattern of the falling rain is beautiful,

and it shows nature's might.

Happy times or sad times, the rain is there throughout,

It's refreshing and brings life, while easily erasing all my doubts.

They cleanse everything I wish they could always stay.

Beautiful rain drops - beautiful rain drops,

washing all the pain away.

They cleanse everything, I wish they could always stay,

I love the calming effect they have on any stormy night or day.

Beautiful rain drops,

Beautiful rain drops,

Beautiful rain drops,

Beautiful rain drops,

washing all the pain away.

Take a Look

Take a look into my soul

& you'll see great despair,

A child inside of an adult's body who just wants you to care.

Take a look into my eyes

& you'll see a kind & loving man,

A father who for his family will struggle

- will fight & always have, over them, a protective hand.

Take a look into my soul

& you'll see anger, but also joy,

The emotions run deep & they're not easy to dismiss or deploy.

Take a look into my eyes

& you'll see a guy who used to be wild & crazy.

That part of me has died

- that's why you haven't seen that side of me lately.

Take a look into my soul,

and you'll see a guy who's learned to turn the other cheek,

I've realized that having a peaceful state of mind is being strong

- not weak.

Take a look into my eyes

& you'll see a survivor from many of life's pains,

I'm a person that sees the many blessings

even though much hell has came.

Take a look into my soul

& see a man with many flaws,

Every person's perfect imperfections are what makes us all.

Take a look into my eyes

& see strength through a life of pain,

Losing loved ones has affected my heart

& I know I'll never be the same.

Take a look into my soul

& you'll see a man who's survived being done foul,

Past pain I've experienced has made me a better person now.

Take a look into my eyes

& you'll see a great determination to do well,

A man who has made many sacrifices & refuses to fail.

Take a look into my soul

& I pray that you'll see a man that has purpose,

One that is here for everyone, so that no one feels worthless.

Take a look into my eyes

& see a man who knows that the bad will be okay,

On any given day - just continue to pray.

Take a look into my soul

& see the will to never quit,

For the many hardships in life, I'm very equipped

& the love I have for all is legit.

Take a look into my eyes

& you'll see a man who knows that hard work is worth it,

One who knows that even though life's a struggle

- he's thankful even though life is never perfect.

Take a look into my soul

& you'll see a writer who's trying to simply inspire,

One whose passion is poetry & it's my one true desire.

Take a look into my eyes

& you'll see a person that's been reborn,

A guy who's lived through having a heart that's scorned

- & has healed from emotions that were once torn.

Glance into my soul

& see a person who is still incomplete,

Stare into my eyes

& see a man who has not yet reached his peak.

There are many levels to me

like there are many pages in a book,

Please take the time to know all parts of me

- please come and take a look.

Whenever You Need Me

I knew you were special, so I tried to resist you
- but then I kissed you.
I'm in love with every hug
- & when you're gone, I truly miss you.
I'll be your protector - your Partner
 - I'll always let your light shine & never try to control you.
When and if, any hard times come - I won't run
- I'll be there to console you.

Love has come to me
when it wasn't something that I was trying to seek,
I tend to be distant & incomplete - but you've given me strength
when I thought I was weak.
My faith in being happy again,
- I have to admit - was extremely bleak.
But you've proved to accomplish an incredible feat
- for a lovely life with you is what I now seek.
You mean so much to my whole existence
- it's those Dimples of yours for me.
You mean so much to my energy
- your precious smile that makes me know we're meant to be.
You have a beautifully infectious touch
- every time it sends chills up & down my spine.
I need you to be all mine - our vibe is one of a kind
- when things get dark you're my sunshine.

You calmed the Storm in my Soul

from too many losses in Love - I need every kiss & every hug.

You always speak life into my Heart

- when I'm with you, I know I'll never be judged.

It's happy Spouse happy House

- so, during times that get worse, we'll put each other first.

My need for you creates a healthy thirst,

- I'm so excited Bae - my emotions are about to burst.

That's why I'll always be around

- this is a forever type of love that we have found,

Whenever You Need me - I'll be there, girl, I swear

 - this connection is Heaven bound.

I wanna hold you & squeeze you

- you put me in a happy place - I love when we embrace,

I didn't want to fall in love again, but now that's the case

- I just wanna wake up every day to your sweet face.

I've started to smile again & it's been such a long while - because I'm healed from past pain & you're the blame,

For me, things will never be the same - into my life you came - and our chemistry is very insane.

From our 1st conversation - to our 1st meet up - to our 1st hug

- I have been completely in love.

You were manifested into my life

- a beautiful Dove from the Most High up above.

It's either you or it's nothing

- you soothe my soul and rid me of all hurt,

You came along and re-established inside of me

what is truly my worth.

You got through to me

when nobody else could reach me,

You're the lesson in love

that I desperately needed someone to teach me.

We are one and that's how we're forever going to be

- our love will never flee,

You're one of a kind & all mine

 - you make me happy & I feel so free.

I made it through all my nightmares

 and now it's only happy days that I see,

You shine brighter than a Sunkissed Crystal.

- I love you April - I'll always be there

- I swear - Whenever You Need Me…..

Hey Ms. Lady

HEY MS. LADY - you're a beautiful sight for me to behold,

I want to conversate with you - get your number - if it's okay for me to be so bold.

I'm interested in seeing how a relationship

with you could unfold,

Just give me a fair shot to initiate things,

or you won't regret not treating me cold.

Please don't take this the wrong way

- Don't be defensive about what I'm about to say,

But I've wanted you in a strong way

- ever since I first saw you that first day.

You probably think it's the temptations of the flesh

& that I only want sex.

But it took courage for me to come

& confess that I believe us being an item is best.

HEY MS. LADY - I could be your protector

- caress you & hold you ever so tight,

Share with each other all our hopes

& dreams while we pillow talk throughout the night.

Let's spend time together growing closer

in a world where too many harsh words are spoken,

We can be each other's positive energy

& pledge to never have any promises broken.

We'll put some drinks on the rocks

- then sip a little while we dance with each other slow,

Falling for each other more & more

as we play old school R&B songs on the radio.

I'll always be true & I see that I'll love being out with you.

Have all kinds of pet names for each other

like bae - baby & boo.

HEY MS. LADY - you'll be my focus in life,

so that way our love could never fade or disappear,

Our connection will get stronger and stronger

and become rock solid through the years.

Our bond will float & be infections

for anyone who's around you and me.

It'll play over and over for everyone to see

- just like an incredibly orchestrated melody.

You'll always come first

- there'll be nothing that comes ahead or above you,

I would happily marvel and be grateful

at the chance to have and to love you.

You can be mine and I'll be there when you need me,

at anytime - a life that's so divine,

A peaceful place is where I'll have your mind

- we'll never be apart - a love so kind.

HEY MS. LADY - when it's times that the unbearable anguish of life's struggles brings us pain,
We'll wash away any hurt we share as our love will sprinkle down as beautiful as the falling rain.
In our combined affection for each other
we can forever shower,
There will be no force on this planet that can stop
how much this love will give us power.
I want to bring peace to your mind
and never bring any type of stress to your head,
I want to be what you dream all night
when you're sleeping in your bed.
Now I'm realistic, so there'll be times we fight
- but don't be alarmed, there'll be no need to cry.
For I'll always be a healing presence
so, you'll never have to dry your eyes.

HEY MS. LADY - our love will never hurt
- so we can just relax and enjoy our time,
And you can be happy I'm yours
and I'll be happy that you're mine.
Together we can build each other up
so that one day we can have it all.
And always have each other's backs
so, when one needs the other, all we have to do is call.

I know you think all men are dogs,

but I can change that thought just come & hold my hand,

I can be your man

& show you many levels of joy

while I'm giving you all that I can.

Our love will be so fresh & pure

- I'll maintain stability & make sure that you're secure.

I'm moving fast, but I had to come

& ask cause life can be sickening

& we'll be each other's cure.

Shattered Pieces

My mind is beginning to go all over the place again,
So instead of leaning on old alcoholic habits
I decided to pick up my notebook and pen.
I'm fighting the temptations of Tanqueray & my thirst for Jack,
I gave up the cups of liquor & its false hope,
because I needed control of my life back.
I'm joyful that I'm blessed,
Although, I need to release some of my everyday stress.
I've made much progress
while I'm surviving many of life's tests.
Being a father is hard, but also a beautiful struggle.
People compliment my parenting,
but I stay humble - dealing with hardships
& still being a role model is very hard to juggle.
I sit & contemplate all the things I have at stake,
I must stay focused on my goals
& I'm sure you all can relate.
I hold on to values that was taught to me as a kid,
And I thank my parents for everything they did
– because they had faith in me
when the faith I had in myself had slid.
Times are getting bold
& its scary watching my life unfold.
I reach for peace,
because dealing with drama has gotten so very old.

No matter how hard I try,

these sad thoughts always enter my mind.

It's so hard for me to unwind

– my anxiety is crippling me all the time.

I hold in my cries for help,

because I'd rather have them go unheard.

The line between happiness

& frustration, for me, has become so blurred.

At times, I can't think straight

& restless nights are back once more,

I can't calm the storm within me

& I fear what my future may have in store.

I can't find any consistency,

although, I really do try.

On the inside, I've started to die

& you can see the confusion in my eyes.

I hate that I'm always out of touch,

I hate that even though I want to satisfy everyone

I'll never really be able to do enough.

I'm only one person & the pressure on me is so unreal,

I hurt from past pain still

& abandonment is what I most often feel.

My mind is never clear & everything for me is dark & hazy,

I swear on my own life that our whole world has gone crazy!!!

I get treated badly when I do good,

but when I act up, I get respect.

My bad points are remembered,

but my good deeds are what people forget.
My life is no longer mine.
I feel like I'm always doing for everyone else,
I'm there when people need me,
but when I need somebody, no one ever helps.
I'm paranoid – hurt & lost,
When it comes to life, I've paid a terrible cost.
Agony & despair are my allies now,
it seems nobody cares, I want to break free,
but I don't know how.
I need time to sit down & figure things out,
I don't know what to do, I'm always left in doubt.
But suddenly, I think of my children again
& I can't leave – disappear or die,
Nobody else is better to teach them
about what to do with their future than I.
I'll teach them to have goals & always stay focused,
I'll show them hope in a world that's so bogus.
I'm going to keep going on,
because many people depend on me,
I'm going to keep on fighting,
although my soul is yearning to be set free.
Feelings of anger & regret, for me, always increases,
I gave my all years ago
& all that's left of me is shattered pieces.

Time and Time Again

Life has always seemed to move really fast for me,
I was somewhat reckless in my later teen-aged years
so, I became a father before I was ready to be.
I was made a leader
before leadership was something I was ready to see,
I feel like I've been playing catch up for like an eternity.
Many setbacks are the reason,
I'm not in the situation I want for my family.
It's so frustrating when your life's plan
& your fate don't ever work together in peaceful harmony.

I'm pretty much sad & happy all of the time,
It's hard keeping positive,
when negative thoughts constantly flood your mind.
It's a struggle keeping a good outlook,
when goodness is hard to find.
It's hard to move forward,
when you've always got things holding you behind.
I get knocked around sideways,
when I'm just trying to keep things in a straight line.
But I do keep faith,
even though I haven't been given a reason,
to have faith or shown a sign.
I have hopeless feelings like I'm stuck in a world
which I don't belong,
I'm a misunderstood, black sheep without a home.

I treat everyone the right way, but I'm constantly done wrong,
I once had hope for the future, but that hope is almost gone.
I hate complaining about this cause it's the same old song,
Days without contentment, for me, seemed so prolonged.
It feels as if unhappiness is my fate,
It hurts that I've lost when I've had so much at stake.
I've fought hard to keep failure from being my trait,
I feel trapped like I'm stuck as sadness' inmate.
My shoulders carry an endlessly heavy weight,
A life that's great is hard for me to anticipate.
I know how it feels when nobody cares,
To be in need of love, but there's nobody there.
When you need someone to take a chance on you
but nobody dares,
When you're judged by your past mistakes & affairs.

I know the heartache of being played like a fool,
To be left behind by someone that you gave your all to.
I've dealt with the frustration of losing
after doing everything you can possibly do,
I've seen the bitterness of defeat that life can hand to you.
I know the pain of losing loved ones that have died,
standing at funerals helplessly watching
everyone around you cry.

I know the struggles of unanswered questions

- you just want to know why.

Plus, I've been a soulless body

although, I have not physically died

- the anguish of life makes it hard to survive.

Because the sad fact is…... I've struggled most of my adult life,

Trying to make the wrong things right.

My insecurities make life a game that's hard for me to win,

They cripple me time & time again.

Symptoms of Being in Love

They stay forever on your mind,
It's that person you just want to wine & dine.
Their presence makes your days kind,
Y'all time together is a sweet divine.
You just need them by your side,
The emotions they bring out of you are such an ecstatic ride.
You just want to be around them,
- you feel without them you'll die.
The sheer beauty of them makes your soul fly.
When you sleep at night, they're the only person you dream of,
These are the symptoms of being in love.
You melt on the inside by just the mention of their name,
You want to shelter them from harm
& shield them from all pain.
You feel blessed, because into your life they finally came,
Nobody else in your life can make you feel the same.
You were once empty inside,
but you now suddenly feel complete.
Your days are filled with joy, when not long ago,
your soul would always weep.
You have an unexpected connection with them
that runs endlessly deep,
Your once quiet emotions now have the will to speak.
It's the freedom of having your feelings rise
like the clouds above,

These are the symptoms of being in love.
You have for each other a mutual desire,
The fact that they're with you keeps you inspired.
Your need for each other's happiness is so very dire,
The passion that you share blazes brighter than any fire.
They are your partner - your heart - your best friend,
Not even in death will the bond you have with them end.
No matter how far apart - in your heart they are there,
It can't be explained how much, for them, you care.
You fit each other perfectly symmetrical
like a hand into a glove,
These are the symptoms of being in love.
Bringing them happiness becomes your duty & craft,
You adore them unconditionally,
because they're your better half.
All the little things they do, make you joyful & even laugh,
You'll do whatever, for them, from the big things to the little -
like running water for their bath.
You're there no matter what, through the thick & thin,
You cherish their whole existence
& with them any battle - war or fight will be a win.
They lift up your spirits & right all the wrongs,
No matter where you may reside
- as long as they're there with you, that is your home.

Your enjoyment comes from the fact
they are all you can think of,
These are the symptoms of being in love.
You try to always keep them overjoyed
& away from days that are sad,
You'll always protect them from darkness' void
& days that are bad.
They are your motivation in any
& everything, that you do,
No matter how far apart physically
- emotionally they'll always be with you.
You're each other's answer when one may not have a clue,
You protect them from all falsehoods & always stay true.
You are finally fulfilled, whereas, you once had felt a void,
Any & all negative misconceptions you had about commitment
have been destroyed.
A wonderful - happily ever after type of life
with them is all you want
& all you can think of.
All of these beautiful things
& many more are the symptoms of being in love.

My Poisonous Downfall

You were supposed to love me forever,

you said you would leave me- never ever.

We were supposed to fight through life together,

You said you would be there through all my life endeavors.

You were supposed to keep my heart from breaking again.

We have fallen apart

- the amount of pain I'm in, should be a sin.

My heart is shattered and there's no bringing it back.

My many colorful, happy emotions

are now sorrow filled and black.

The amount of agony I'm in is unmatched,

Anger & pain have come on to me in a full-blown attack.

My emotions are dark and bitterly cold,

My youthful spirit is now brittle and old.

Life sadly goes on,

all the while, I'm left no longer feeling strong.

I'm numb - all my feelings are gone,

I lock myself in my home and turn off my phone.

I've been harshly let down,

nothing but the rain of unforgiving pain is around.

Happy days are no longer here,

It's impossible for my mind to be clear.

I have clouded thoughts of regret,

our past life together is what I want to forget.

Old memories that once were happy now irritate my soul,

I just want to let these thoughts go.

You let what others had to say drive you away,

you abandoned me when I needed you to stay.

This whole situation has ripped my insides apart,

I can no longer feel my heart.

I've got this empty feeling in my chest,

I was once so confident and now I'm an insecure mess.

I've been hurt to the point of insanity,

You're so heartless - how could you do this to me?

We were supposed to be a family,

this huge amount of agony should have never ever come to be.

Way too many times, I wasted my time on all of your nonsense,

Way too many times, I stressed my mind about you

and you were not worth all that suspense.

I swear I now hate you, after I once loved you with all my soul.

I swear I hate the fact,

that my most intimate secrets are something that you know.

You took advantage of me & left me vulnerable,

because I was far too kind,

You used me as your fool

and played many games with my mind.

Your claims of love for me were deceitfully false,

the loving person I once was, is now forever lost.

It was you I wanted to stay with

& I thought you wanted to stay with me too,

I'm stuck in a sad abyss because I placed too much trust in you.

I was happy with the hold you had on me

and you viciously let go of your grip,

You wanted to go on without me and sadly you got your wish.

Broken - mad and sad I am, because you were all I had.

You've hurt me so bad

by taking away a love that had once left me glad.

My hopes have been selfishly cut off and taken,

& the faith I had in our love has been defeated and shaken.

I can't push away none of my thoughts of regret,

I can't stand tall anymore - my life without you is such a wreck.

How you got me to this point,

I don't think I'll ever be able to recall.

You blindsided me

- our complete fallout is something that I never saw.

I'm bruised and weakened

- I can no longer deal with any more of this anguish at all.

You're my biggest failure - my venom

- my painfully poisonous downfall.

-

Chapter 4: Montre's Memoirs

My middle daughter, Peyton & I

Working On the Frontline (2020)

Year 2020 & it's got me sitting here taking shots of Vodka

I'm so stressed & pissed,

But it ain't enough liquor in the whole wide world

that's able to stop a pain like this.

2020 - I done seen way too much agony

& we've barely made it out of the year,

They went & murdered my lil Cousin Josh

& it's got me still crying real tears.

2020 - It was so hard for me to keep losing the people

that for my whole life I have loved,

And now I've got these doctors telling me

 that the Corona Virus took my Uncle Junebug.

2020 - and cancer was & is still real

- and Stephanie's death is a hurt that I still feel.

She was one of the kindest souls

that I was lucky enough to meet - her energy can't be killed.

My mother-in- law passed

& the hurt from it has my heart racing

 - the sound of it is so loud,

How the HELL could death just come

& take Mama Dawana away? 2020 was so unfair & wild.

I was naive to think that love alone is enough

to create a perfect fit like a horse to carriage.

Lack of communication & my long hours working

on the frontline has destroyed my marriage.

I drive city buses for a living

- so I'm working on the frontline

& trust me I've seen a whole lot,

It's depressing but I got daughters to support

- so me working on the frontline isn't going to stop.

Working on the frontline

- where the Streets are empty

because the city is under quarantine.

It's crazy seeing parks & pools caution taped off

like it's a murder scene.

Working on the Frontline

- where everyone is wearing latex gloves

& Masks around their face,

People are on edge and extremely paranoid

all while trying not to catch a Covid-19 case.

Working on the frontline

- where restaurants & stores are closed

or only giving limited service.

It's now too dangerous to go outside

& everything is on hold until further notice.

Working on the frontline

if you cough people look at you

like you did something menacing.

The paranoia is real

you must stay 6 ft. away from each other……

maintain social distancing.

Working on the frontline

- where it seems that this new "normal" is sadly here to stay.

And everyday the bad news keeps coming

- I just want all this chaos to end & go away.

I promise 2020 was absolutely the worst year ever

& it's hard for me to clear my mind,

It's impossible to unwind

- too much has happened all at once, so peace is hard to find.

I feel backed into a corner I don't know where I'm headed

- I feel like I'm walking blind,

I'm just glad I made it out of 2020

& I hope I don't die

- while still working on the frontline.

You Said Goodbye

You said goodbye…..
We were supposed to be all that each other needed or had,
A life partnership is what we did - how did it all end so bad?
You said that you were too late to be my first
but you were gonna be my last.
You were special to me - a dream come true
- but now we're another love story that ended sad.
It started out so beautifully
- or so it seemed that way to me - so tender loving & great,
But somewhere down the line - the love had me blind
- cause it ended in a much different fate.
A connection was made & love was born
so I'm torn on what I needed to do,
I always thought we would be forever
- but now we talk almost never - I can't believe I lost you.
It hurts not having you
- I'm moving on, but I'm in so much pain
- I gave you my last name,
I still can't fully connect on exactly what happened
or how our end even came.
You said that we were gonna become one
- so this split has hurt me in a way that's the worse,
But I still love LOVE even though LOVE for me
always seems to hurt.

We just became yet another tragically sad love story,
I still remember the days when you actually did adore me.
But things began changing once we both got older
- We drifted apart instead of getting closer.
You said you hated when I drank
- but I got to the point that I only felt normal
when I wasn't sober.

I completely hate the fact that for you I still do care
- it's so unfair.
I hate that I'm even writing this,
but the lack of closure is killing my soul - so I had to share.
I promised myself that all this won't define me,
so this is the last time on this subject I will speak.
I pulled out my pen & paper
so that all my pinned-up frustrations can finally come out & leak.
You said I worked too much,
but I was just trying to get us where we needed to be.
The fate of us being together was just not meant to be
- I truly thought you believed in me.
I guess cause I was at work a whole lot, you just assumed
I no longer had a care,
Just because it's not seen - doesn't mean it's not there.
I thought you would match my energy
- I gave my all - but that's something you didn't see,
I didn't realize you weren't happy
- so I can definitely understand why you wanted to be free.

True intentions & true colors are revealed everyday all the time,
So I never should have allowed myself to walk around colorblind.
I got disrespected a lot during the climax of our relationship.
I hated the way we ended,
such a horrible sudden stop to something
that started out so splendid.
I'm very thankful that you gave me two beautiful daughters
and that's something I can't deny,
I'm tired of people asking me what happened to us
cause I'm not really able to explain why.
I've found some peace inside my soul since you left
- so there was some healing in those tears I had to cry
- we never did see eye to eye.
You said you just needed a lil space, but that was a lie
- cause as soon as you moved out you had someone else
- so I guess it really was best that you said goodbye.

Demons Chasing Me

Expectations are always so high
- I wish people didn't see me as they do,
If they only knew that demons chase me every day,
but for me this news isn't brand new.

I take the stress on without showing the hurt
that I have inside - I drown it with my pride,
I hold it all inside.
- I know I shouldn't, but I do and I honestly don't know why.
I never have a peace of mind
- happiness is what I need fate to come to me and bring.
Sadness is such a terrible thing
- the depression grabs my soul & doesn't allow it to sing.

I'm surrounded by so much
but I still remain in pain - feeling outcasted and lonely.
It's so much out here that's fake & phony
- I only see things getting worse - this is my testimony.
My mood is dim I'm always feeling so low
- I need help but I have absolutely nowhere to go,
I've lost so many that were close to me
& each death hurts - so many devastating blows.

I swallow all the anguish

- this could make a grown man cry

& I truly want to die.

I medicate my insomnia through my alcoholic habits

& that's how I make it and get by.

I worry about my babies,

because they are inheriting a planet that is completely crazy.

The future is unclear and hazy

because I doubt they can make it in a world that's so shady.

My world is as dark as it could be

- a sign of hope never comes for me to see,

Fighting depression is a never-ending battle for me,

everyday feels like agony.

I miss lost loved ones gone

& I want to keep their legacy alive - I'm trying

- but inside I'm dying.

Then I start to use strength from within

- to never give in despite my soul crying.

Though suffering from a bleeding heart

- I refuse to let that rip me apart.

Regaining a healthy mind state to control my fate

& to stay the happy soul, I was from the start.

Even though the hurt will still be here

- I will push forward throughout my remaining years.

Fighting through any pain

& tears to be a good example to all family

& friends that I hold dear.

I'll be the voice for souls that died

- being a reincarnation & new hope for my whole nation,

This is for all lost souls without a destination

- they'll now have a location.

I want my determination to reach the whole population

& every generation,

It's gonna be such a sensation

to beat depression's hopeless demonstrations.

I'll be sure to keep my mind negative free

for being perfect is impossible to be,

I'll always strive to be a strong example for all people to see,

That I'm a force to be reckoned with

- even with all these demons chasing me.

So Many Unanswered Questions

How come having a good heart gets you treated so badly?
Why is it that many times the result of being in love
ends so sadly?
How come people tend to get punished for doing the right thing?
Why has it been so hard for us to carry out Dr. King's dream?
How come our world allows so much pain and disease?
Why is it that it seems the Lord never hears our pleas?
How come it's easier to walk away
instead of fighting the good fight?
Why has it been so hard for me to see all the good in life?
How come when I close my eyes, I see nothing but pain?
Why is our world so crazy?
- so many good deeds are done in vain.
How come our Lord allows so much murder and even suicide?
Why does violence have to be the way so many have died?
How come tears shed can't instantly ease the pain in one's heart
Why does it seem when hate is around love falls apart?
How come when you're reliable, people try to take advantage?
Why is it that a good peace of mind is so hard to manage?
How come it is so hard to tell people's true intentions for you?
Why is trusting someone something that's so hard to do?

How come a happy medium in life is so hard to juggle?
Why is it that life has to be such a struggle?
How come past love shown can't always be there?
Why is it such an uphill battle finding people who actually care?
How come our fellow people are constantly treating each other
so vicious and mean?
Why is it that most good things in life are never
as good as they seem?
How come as an adult the innocence
you had as a child seems so far away and gone?
Why does road to redemption have to be so long?
How come we are left so lost and confused many times?
Why is it so hard to rid stress from all our minds?
How come life beats us down in such an unbearable way?
Why is it when you're honest and real,
many never want to hear what you have to say?
How come those you hold dear tend to be the ones you lose?
Why is it in life the hard decisions aren't easier to choose?
How come I'm such a restless soul? - I really want to know.
Why is it that my mind can't let past losses and failures go?
For that very reason and many more I've cut way down on my
alcohol intake as of late,
I need a clear mind and you can't achieve that
if you're always in a drunken mind-state.
Through all my heartaches - my frustrations & my laughter
- my life has taught me many valuable lessons.
But I'm still a tortured soul
- that's full of so many unanswered questions.

Beautifully Black

I apologize because I took for granted
all the sacrifices that were made for me,
I didn't realize all the blood that was shed
so that I could stand here and be free.
I apologize because I haven't been grateful enough,
for the freedom I have to express my mind,
I didn't realize all the fighting it took
just to have the chance to recite this piece at this time.
I apologize because for the many times
I was too lazy to live up to my potential,
I didn't realize all the struggle that took place
so I could be in position to learn & display my credentials.

I hope that my awakening shows
that those sacrifices weren't made in vain,
I will always stand tall and strive towards being great
for my people have endured plenty of pain.
I hope that through the heartache and tears shed
that much pride can be shown now.
I will always be strong
& I'll always have strength
because my ancestors showed me how.
I hope that I can carry on a legacy
that was established way before my existence came to be.

I will always value our rise from slavery – Jim Crow Laws &
unjustified white supremacy.
I'm in debt to them all
and it's a debt that could never ever be fully paid.
So I'm here to say that much respect is given to them
& my quest to honor them has forever stayed.
I'm the anger of a slave who was shackled for far too long,
So I'll always remember the anguish
they went through and the pain still lives on.
I'm a descendent of Kings and Queens
& it seems our royalty is something I forgot.
I was wrong for not always realizing this,
my nonchalant behavior in this matter now will stop.

It's Martin's dream and Malcolm's purpose
that our equality would become a reality.
We're far more than what our beginnings
of being forced away from home suggested that we'd be.
It's why Mandela withstood imprisonment,
because the fight against oppression must always continue,
We're beautiful & our existence like everyone else's is necessary
- that's why their spirit lives in me & you.
It's why we get so frustrated,
because we're not 3rd eye blind
so we can see our world being racist.
We're a proud race & at times it's misunderstood,
because it isn't always shown on a regular basis.

I hope to be a positive movement that never stops

for my people & everyone else.

I struggled to write these words only ,

because I so desperately just want to help.

I hope to uplift, love everyone

& continue to bring pride to my black nation,

I struggled to write this because I'm trying to be fair even though

we haven't been treated fairly in many situations.

I hope this hits powerfully

because too many times great messages get lost.

I struggled to write this,

but I want to show that my love for my people

will be here at any cost.

I apologize & for now on I'll never take for granted

what all it took for us to try to live equally.

I hope you can sincerely see my love and respect

for our existence to be.

I'm in debt forever to my elders,

because they paved the way for me.

It's the past I will never forget

for without it the future is impossible to see.

I hope these thoughts touch you all

& I hope many years after my demise these words

can be what many can foresee.

For this is my heartfelt tribute to the beauty of Black History.

I love LOVE & I hate HATE

I love LOVE & I hate HATE,

They both go hand & hand

& in the end they both can cause different fates.

I love LOVE & I hate HATE,

Many say hate's a wasted emotion.

While love is what we wish to share with our mates.

I love LOVE & I hate HATE,

Love will always last through the evil destruction

-hate's earthquake.

I love LOVE & I hate HATE,

Love is hard to find these days,

but it is worth the wait.

I love LOVE & I hate HATE,

Hate drowns people's happiness

& it's such a waste.

I love LOVE & I hate HATE,

Love is the strength you need when life

puts too much hate on your plate.

I love LOVE & I hate HATE,

Love will comfort you in life when you have a lot at stake.

I love LOVE & I hate HATE,

Always push hate to the side,

because joy is what love makes.

I love LOVE & I hate HATE,

Love will show you who's real & hate always exposes the fake.

I love LOVE & I hate HATE,

Hate abandons you.

While love always carries its own weight.

I love LOVE & I hate HATE,

Hate often will tempt you but don't ever take hate's bait.

I love LOVE & I hate HATE,

Love gives you a natural high.

While hate causes a terrible mind state.

I love LOVE & I hate HATE,

Hate leaves you miserable.

While love gives joy you can't even rate.

I love LOVE & I hate HATE,

Hate causes confusion while love sets things straight.

I love LOVE & I hate HATE,

Hate destroys lives.

While love sets them on a path that can be great.

I love LOVE & I hate HATE,

Hate comes from the fires below.

While love is waiting for us at Heaven's gates.

I love LOVE & I hate HATE,

Hate is evil.

While love's unconditional

– a fact that many won't debate.

I love LOVE & I hate HATE,

The hate in our world is a roadblock.

While love always accommodates.

I love LOVE & I hate HATE,

Hate leads to failure.

While love leads you to a destination that is great.

I love LOVE & I hate HATE,

Love sets you free.

While hate traps you as its inmate.

I love LOVE & I hate HATE,

Love is pure.

While hate causes pain and confusion to inflate.

I love LOVE & I hate HATE,

Hate brings agony.

While feelings of being ecstatic

 & overjoyed are love's trait.

I love LOVE & I hate HATE,

These are just my thoughts & I pray you all can relate.

Refuse all hate because love is what we should await.

My appreciation for LOVE is what I am trying to translate,

because I will always love LOVE & I will always hate HATE.

Her Precious Pearl

I love being in her angelic & juicy presence,

The feeling of her is happiness in its purest essence.

I caress her & rub her lightly,

I'm going to give her pleasure by invoking some pain slightly.

All night it's going to last,

I go slow, then go fast - I keep going & make her splash.

The expression on her face when I put it in is priceless,

The way she glides on it & moans lets me know she likes it.

She grabs the back of my head while I French kiss & eat her,

she digs her nails in my back as I push inside of her joy deeper.

I grind inside her and dig it all against her walls,

Her wetness comes & drenches me like a waterfall.

I love being in her, skin to skin,

The pleasure she invokes is far too angelic to be a sin.

It's pure Heaven as I continue to keep stroking her,

Passionate love making with her every night is going to occur.

Flowing & swimming in her wet & deep ocean,

Sweating & moaning as our connection has her open.

I push & dig - this is an ecstasy type of physical joy,

Our beautiful bodies are magical

- our lust to touch is what we both enjoy.

Rubbing & lusting we keep on busting,

Gridding & squeezing each other keeps our juices rushing.

We go again & again we keep wanting more.

Connecting our bodies as one, makes a nice sight

- every night this is what we have in store.

Her legs wrap around me & bound me,

She arches her back as her peak has found me.

I stay inside her as she grips & scratches,

I thrust all in her from behind

- I stay in awe each time our bodies attaches.

The chemistry we have is so breathtaking - loving & exciting,

I love every moment from - the trusting to the biting.

Sliding in & out I don't ever want to stop or quit,

We keep going past our peaks

because when it comes to ultimate physical pleasure this is it.

The passion rolled up in each other bodies we let just unfurl,

Our fluids come together in a sensual swirl.

Against each other's bodies we both push & hurl,

Lips are bitten - hard breaths are taken & toes curl.

This is our sexy dance - together we both twirl,

It's completely heaven for me

- each time I enter her Precious Pearl.

POETRY is Me

My words will make you cry & make you smile,

I hope my message spreads for many miles.

Poetry helps me soothe my brain,

It helps me express my pain.

The words & phrases just pop into my head,

It happens anytime whether I'm out & about or laying in bed.

I write about everything funny or deep,

I put all my hurt & love on my notebook sheets.

I write about all my long days,

I write to loved ones that God called away.

I write stories & use great detail,

I love writing - I hope that you all can tell.

I write about the ups & downs,

I write about the joy I've found.

I express all my sadness,

I share with you all my madness.

Turn my notebook pages & they show every heartache,

My notebook pages show every heartbreak.

I write my love for my little girls and boy,

My kids give me so much joy.

I write about being so stressed,

but God gave me life, so I know I'm blessed.

I don't need the liquor in my cup,

I can make it because I have family that loves me very much.

I keep writing because it brings my soul power,

The words are my seeds & my poems are my flower.

Oh, dear poetry, I found love the day I met you,

The day I met poetry, I knew I found a love that was true.

I love expression, it makes me as happy as I can be,

I am POETRY & POETRY is me.

Poetry is Me (Part 2)

I never could rap & I never could sing - but it's a beautiful thing - when I've got a paper & pen & we begin to blend. I never could dance & I never could perform - but it's a perfect storm - when my poetic mind state creates thoughts that others can read & relate.

The exploration of my mind - over any amount of time - brings you TRE'S Thoughts & poetic rhymes. So, everyone please come along - this is my dance & my song - it'll be an incredible ride for you all that'll last very long.

It's a love between lovers - the bond between sisters & brothers - and for me there simply can't be any other. It's like my Grandma's love that floats like a feather - but can survive all bad weather - this connection will last forever.

My passion for it will always be true - it's my gift. I was blessed with & I'm sharing it with you - it's all that I ever wanted to do. It's within my soul & it has no bounds - it's the reason for the inner peace that I have found - this is my truth & my need for it is profound.

Happiness can be so hard to find - we live in a World that is beyond unkind - so being in a poetic mindset is how I unwind. In a World that's hard for us to trust - it's a connection much deeper than lust - that's why I take my time with it because it's far too precious to rush.

I look in my baby girl's eyes & realize everything's gonna be alright - I'll keep fighting through my fears & always do what's right - my bond with my children will always be tight. I just haven't been myself lately so retreating to writing is what I decided to do - no matter what I may go through - Poetry I owe everything to you.

It's all those ecstatic, happy days from so many yesterdays ago that is what's truly missed, So I grab my pen & write about them as I reminisce - remembering a time that was bliss. My mind is a Masterpiece painting vivid pictures for everyone to see - my peace of mind comes from being able to express myself & that's what's key - Forever We are Poetry & thankfully, Poetry is me.

It's my life - it's my MOVEMENT - it's a ton of talented Poets that write, but I was born 2 do this. It feels so right - it can't be wrong - It reminds me of some of my favorite Jayceon Taylor AKA The Game songs: I sit alone - at home - in the zone - just trying to write classics - because We are Poetry & thankfully, Poetry is me.

I Grab My Pen

I grab my pen & use it to express my anguish and despair,
I grab my pen & use it to express happiness in my heart
when good feelings are there.
I grab my pen & use it to express the thoughts
in every angle of my mind,
I grab my pen & it helps me through depression every time.
I grab my pen & it helps set me free,
I grab my pen & the thoughts that I have many other people can
now see.
I grab my pen & now my words can last forever,
I grab my pen and it always makes the hard times better.
I grab my pen because its more powerful than any drug,
I grab my pen to extinguish hate & spread love.
I grab my pen & it tells my unheard story,
I grab my pen & it shows a poetic mind state in all its glory.
I grab my pen & it helps me to spread the truth,
I grab my pen, so when I'm dead & gone
& if my presence is needed, here's the proof.
I grab my pen & the ink spills onto paper
and a masterpiece is born,
I grab my pen & it mends pains that had my emotions torn.
I grab my pen & it represents every writer that ever existed,
I grab my pen & feelings that were locked deep
are no longer restricted.

I grab my pen & love lost doesn't hurt as much anymore,

I grab my pen & facing my fears is what I start to explore.

I grab my pen & it flows expressing my blood sweat & tears,

I grab my pen to give everyone a voice

that will last for years & years.

I grab my pen & it give hopeless situations hope,

I grab my pen & help those hurting to be able to cope.

I grab my pen & my heavy heart feels much lighter now,

I grab my pen & and it's no longer so hard to smile.

I grab my pen & I'm reminded that no matter what,

I can make it,

I grab my pen & I know, no matter how hard it gets in life,

I can take it.

I grab my pen because those happy days

from many yesterdays ago is what I miss,

I grab my pen to write about those days & reminisce.

I was feeling inspired today, so I chose to write again,

No matter what happens to me through writing,

I can always win.

I put all my thoughts out there, so my soul can stay cleansed,

My love for all is real

- and it's shown every time I grab my pen......

Chapter 5: Demontre's Dissertation

My youngest daughter, Raegan

The Most Beautiful Woman That I've Ever Seen

She's the most beautiful woman that I've ever seen,

And if you've ever been in love

then you know exactly what I mean.

She's so loving & sweet - so unbelievably kind,

She's my love - my motivation - in darkness, she's my sunshine.

I'd lost faith in love & she came

& put love back inside of my heart & mind,

We are unstoppable when we have our goals in life combined.

A blessing is what she is to me

- needed my hope in love restored & she was that sign,

So, my loyalty to what we have will never decline.

She's the most beautiful woman that I've ever seen,

And if you've ever been in love

then you know exactly what I mean.

I'm head over heels over her - my love is very true,

Rubbing - loving & kissing on her is all I want to do.

Complete happiness is what she brings me

& these are the feelings I'm sharing with all of you,

All I need is her - our connection is all that's in my view.

She's all mine & I'm all hers

- this is something no one will misconstruc.

The natural high she gives me

isn't something that you can subdue.

She's the most beautiful woman that I've ever seen,

And if you've ever been in love

then you know exactly what I mean.

I love making love to her

- throughout the years, the passion is still there,

I'm ecstatic at the fact that after

so much time we're still a happy pair.

Her beauty still has me in awe

- when she walks by, I can't help but to stop & stare,

I'm addicted to every single ounce of her tender love & care.

She can have all of me- I will go with her anywhere,

She's so adorable - it's a timeless love bond that we share.

She's the most beautiful woman that I've ever seen,

And if you've ever been in love

then you know exactly what I mean.

I'm so ecstatically happy

when she's away, it's her presence that I anticipate,

Those who have felt this type of bond

I know can positively relate.

She brings a joyous warmth to my whole mental mind state,

Nothing short of a happily ever after

ending with her is what I await.

She always has my back

- all my needs she's willing to accommodate,

My heart beats for her & that'll never be up for debate.

She's the most beautiful woman that I've ever seen,

And if you've ever been in love

then you know exactly what I mean.

I'm her left hand & she's my right - we're an unbreakable team,

She's lovely - nothing short of a true dream.

Any support she needs, it's my shoulder she can come to & lean,

She brightens my soul when you look into my eyes

you can see it gleams.

So, if you've ever been in love

then you know exactly what I mean - she's my everything,

She's my whole world

- The Most Beautiful Woman that I've Ever Seen.

Two Insecure Souls

I'm obsessed with her, and she's obsessed with me,
As far as I'm concerned, we'll be together for an eternity.
I'm not going to lie & say it was love at first sight,
But it was a strong attraction between us,
when we met that first night.
Whether our relationship is healthy or not isn't our concern,
We are forever until we reach Heaven
or go to hell together & burn.
Our whole existence is stained with our blood,
our sweat and our tears,
The pain we inflict on each other is just a form of our love
that'll be shared through the years.
I take her for granted and she's never appreciated me,
We hold on even though it's unhealthy, as you can clearly see.
We stay frustrated in love with a bond that is strained,
I stay in a lovely lust with her although my heart is pained.
We have for each other an uncomfortable thirst,
She's the greatest and the best at being the worst.
I take advantage of her many times over,
Just to deal with all this we pretty much don't stay sober.
Call it drunk in love or high and alive either way it doesn't matter,
When this ride is done, we'll have collapsed lungs - a damaged liver and a useless bladder.

So much pain between us has been afflicted,
Cheating - beating and any affection between us
tends to be restricted.
We love and hate each other, and our emotions stay conflicted,
Our love is baffling to others and leaves people
confused and twisted.
Our hearts have been broken by each other
our painful connection is very clear,
But it seems we won't see the light until one day when the
essence of our presence disappears and is no longer here.
I'm staying because I can't live without her,
Even though all my frustrating thoughts have been about her.
This damning hate type of love is unreal,
Feelings of being lost and vulnerable are what we both feel.
Our teardrops drip like blood running from a deep cut,
We are so wounded from each other, the agony we've caused is
just simply too much.
The hate we share is aggressive and can't be contained,
But when I'm desperate for any attention,
she's there so I can't complain.
The devilish emotions we have are a sickness,
but our physical pleasure is angelic and Heaven sent.
We've never been straight forward about our unhappiness,
the line that separates the good and bad is horrifically bent.
We're psychotic together but we'll be suicidal apart,
We're poison for each other's hearts

- we've been like this from the start.

Our first kiss was outstanding, and my mind is still blown away

from our first sexual encounter,

I've been addicted to being mistreated

since the day that I found her.

The bitter and cold feelings I give her is what she holds inside,

The resentment and regret we share is something

that always gets pushed to the side.

We are two dead roses whose combined

misery is what's keeping our love alive,

Two insecure souls who are stuck together

until we eventually die.

Don't try to understand this, it's just the way we are,

There's no way to get out

because we're stuck in this abyss way too far.

We are two bleeding souls with hearts full of scars,

Two bloody roses whose shine is dim

as if we were a pinch black star.

Whether our relationship is healthy or not isn't our concern,

We are forever until we reach Heaven

or go to hell together & burn.

I'm not going to lie & say it was love at first sight,

But it was a strong attraction between us

when we met that first night.

I'm obsessed with her, and she's obsessed with me,

As far as I'm concerned, we'll be together for an eternity.

Stuck in love - stuck in hate - stuck with nowhere to go,

As two dead roses - as Two Insecure Souls.

Two Victims DEAD

He's a married man and she knows this,
His wife caught them before, but they still didn't quit.
They would walk hand in hand,
She loved her time with someone else's man.

This woman is sleeping with somebody's husband,
And even worse his wife is her cousin!!!
They're both hurting her, but in her face, they smile,
This whole situation is just so foul.

They knew what they had done was a sin,
They promised her it wouldn't ever happen again.
She stayed with her husband after they got caught,
They swore that the affair would stop.

But now they're secretly back at it,
They fiend for each other like addicts.
His wife can feel that somethings going down,
There are rumors floating all over town.

They keep sneaking around and now people are talking,
They were so bold - they were seen at the park together walking.
They are killing her- and they don't even realize,
They are killing her - you can see it in her eyes.

But this time she's done,
She goes and gets her husband's gun.
Not respecting others can make a small situation bigger,
She ran into their hotel room and pulled the trigger.

She shot them as they laid in bed,
She was so angry; all she saw was red.
The very next day all the newspapers said,
A WOMAN ARRESTED - A DOUBLE HOMICIDE,
TWO VICTIMS DEAD

Death

No matter what - from it there is no escape,

No matter what - it will be every one of our fates.

It comes in so many different forms and so many different ways,

It is the end, many of people's nights and or their days.

IT IS DEATH.

It could happen today, or 1,000 weeks from tomorrow,

And when it comes, it will leave tons of heartfelt sorrow.

It preys on the young and dumb

and the ones who live to be wise and old,

Its grip is sudden - swift and bold.

IT IS DEATH.

It is in wars that don't have a place,

It takes all of us no matter your age or race.

Now if you cause it, it is against the law,

But no matter what it's going to get us all.

IT IS DEATH.

It is going to come in due time,

I often worry that it's my soul it's going to find.

It takes away the strong - the weak - the sane and the crazy,

It snatches away the grown and even our innocent babies.

IT IS DEATH.

You never know what will be its plan,

I know I don't ever want to feel its unforgiving hand.

When it comes, you see so many cry,

When it comes, people say it'll be alright, but that's a lie.

IT IS DEATH.

It is there when there's violence,

And it always brings silence.

In the game we call "Life" it will always win,

No matter what its streak will never end.

IT IS DEATH.

It doesn't care about all the hurt it has made,

It's taken away so many we wished could have stayed.

Even though I can't stop it - I hope it never comes,

And when it does come, I know my life will be truly done.

You just never know when you may inhale

then exhale your last breath,

You just never know when you're going to eventually

meet your DEATH.

Please stay forever blessed........

A Fair Chance

I didn't want the women that was close,

so I traveled miles and miles to be right by their door.

I took rejection so many times and yet I still went back for more.

I didn't want the women that seemed "boring"

even though they were the ones that was respected,

Instead, I foolishly ran for the women

who were always dressed half naked.

I kept chasing the women who didn't want me

because the thought of moving on, I just didn't understand,

I kept trying to be more - even though

I was often put in the zone to only be a friend.

I would keep on trying, although it was obvious

that we wouldn't cross that line,

I pushed away many good ones

who could've made my life divine.

I gave attention to the ones who flirted

and only played games with my mind,

It's embarrassing to look back on this

because I wasted so much time.

Young and dumb, I played the role of such a fool,

I went so hard for the ones that weren't about much

and that just wasn't cool.

I took chances for ones that wasn't deserving

& I only went for them because their beauty caught my eye,

Even though ugly on the inside - just a small amount of attention

from them made me feel as if I could fly.

A perfect connection can come no matter how much
they do or don't have outside beauty,
You must choose the ones that will cherish you
as if it's their duty.
I dealt with the aggravation many times over and over again,
I keep trying to push and force my way in
- but it wasn't a battle that was meant for me to win.
I wasn't wanted no matter what I thought I had to do,
I just didn't want to see the light and see what was true.
I needed to see that it wasn't meant to be,
Setting myself up for failure seemed to be my destiny.
Life's too short to continue to force the unknown,
You must see the signs when those signs are shown.
I kept going for the wrong girl, but I've now learned my lesson,
I kept going for the wrong girl & it caused me so much stressing.
I used to be so shallow, and because of that,
I used to miss out on what would've been a blessing,
I just wasn't mature enough then and now this is my confession.
This is my apology for the good ones who got pushed away,
Those were dark times for me - I was full of so much play.
I've come a long way I really must say,
I've learned that you must be ready to appreciate it when a good
woman comes into your life one day.
No more chasing and running around town all crazy,
You must respect and love when you have a good lady.
Then it will be magical, when you have your first kiss
and first dance,
It's a beautiful sight when you give love a fair chance.

Please Still Love Me

It doesn't matter if you're my sister or my brother,
If you're my friend or my lover.
Happiness is what I need to see,
Please still love me.
It doesn't matter when or where,
I just want you to always care.
Joyful days is what I want my life to be,
Please still love me.
Let me inside your heart,
Nothing will ever make us part.
I've seen too much pain so hear my plea,
Please still love me.
I'm not perfect I make many mistakes,
To fix them, I'll do whatever it takes.
Stand by me and don't ever flee,
Please still love me.
On days hard times has got us low,
On days we are lost with nowhere to go.
These are the times being positive is the key,
Please still love me.
On nights we might fight,
On days that I'm wrong and you are right.
Don't argue and start acting ugly,
Please still love me.

If you're depressed, use my shoulder to cry,

Love and hate go hand in hand, but I'm not sure why.

I'll be your crutch indefinitely,

Please still love me.

There are days when life hurts,

There are days when we all will doubt our worth.

But we're all beautiful notes in life's symphony,

Please still love me.

As I sit and write you this letter,

I hope and pray that bad days end up better.

Although our world drives us so very crazy,

Please still love me.

We've all lost people that death took away,

We mourn our losses every day.

When I die, I hope to live in the skies above me,

And please - Oh please - still love me.

Free (Longer Version)

I need those once happy days to come back upon me
- I just wanna be..... FREE.

Free from pain - free from hurtful memories in my Brain.
Free from Stress - why does Life have to be such a Test?

Free from Depression, it's very sad to behold - my heart was warm, but now it's cold.
Free from all this dreadful hate - free from those who only discriminate.

I need those once happy days to come back upon me
- I just wanna be..... FREE.

Free from the agony of being rejected - free from the anger you get when you get disrespected.
Free from disappointing letdowns - free from loneliness & feeling hellbound.

Free from the emptiness of abandonment - free from self-doubt - No matter what happens I can handle it.
Free from all the pressure, when it's just too much - free from the anguish I feel from loved ones lost by death's touch.

I need those once happy days to come back upon me
- I just wanna be..... FREE.

Free from all of the bad energy - I swear it feels as if it's surrounding me.
Free from not being able to view things clearly - I know it's there, but it's so hard to see.

Free from all of these cloudy thoughts - I am so unsure
- I need to find confusion's cure.
Free the shackles of feeling so defeated all the time - I have a hurt soul and shattered mind.

Free from all of my uncertainty - Life has been hurting me
- but I know what my journey is supposed to be,

I need those once happy days to come back upon me
- I just wanna be…. FREE……………………………………….

A Mind Full of Ideas That's Locked

I have so many words & ideas
that's flowing throughout my head,
I want to write & express them,
but the ideas stay in my mind instead.
So many stories & rhyme schemes
but my hunger to release them right now won't be fed,
I've got a thirst to release my thoughts,
but my creative writing skills seem to be currently dead.
I try to force out my ideas,
but they lay locked up & I can't find the key,
I want to express myself with a great piece, but tonight
I can't find the words to make my vision something you can see.
A poetic mind state has been my gift, but this time a beautiful
poetic expression just isn't meant to be,
I've been a wordsmith throughout the years, but on this night
a nice flowing piece seems to have escaped me.
The voices that go unheard can usually be found in my written
expressions,
Detailed stories & real-life situations have been explained
through me because writing has been my blessing.
I have written stories of mystery & suspense
- & I have kept people guessing,
But on this night, I'm completely stuck
& sadly that goes without question.

I haven't written anything in a while & this is the reason why,
Life has been moving so fast for me lately, so it's been hard for me to just let my thoughts fly.
An uninspired night has come,
so I'm just randomly writing this to make the time go by,
Writer's block can be such a curse, it's so crazy how an active mind can just shut down & die.
I've always strived to stay inspired - even reading dictionaries
& thesauruses to make my vocabulary tighter
- just so I can become a better writer.
Days & nights like this are the worse,
I'm haunted by the curse of Writer's Block,
I can't seem to release because I have a Mind full of Ideas that's locked.
I can't think of anything creative this straining is starting to make my mind ache & pound,
I'm filled up with all kinds of thoughts, but on this night I can't find the right words to write down.
I start to put ideas together, but they soon become jumbled
& I start to fumble them around,
The way I want the words to flow is difficult tonight
- a consistent flow just hasn't been found.
I'm frustrated because I'm stuck on what I'm trying to say,
I hate trying to write when the words keep falling short like they are on this day.

I need to focus & collect my thoughts,

but it feels this writer's block is here to stay,

I need to clear my mind & just flow,

but this writer's block has kicked in & it won't go away.

Everything is so unclear now,

you can see the anguish is all in my face,

Being unable to complete my thoughts has left me in an uncomfortable place.

The words are running away from me

- I can't catch up, as if I'm stuck in a losing race,

I was once a poetic ace, but at this time it feels I have fallen from Grace.

Tonight's struggle has brought me some aggravation,

or can I just call it a Poet's blues,

The ideas are just not flowing out of my mind

like they used to do.

I'm my biggest critic

& this is going to cause me a lot of self-ridicule,

I'm trapped in a wordless abyss.

 – Therefore, this is the piece I'm left to give to you.

I've always strived to stay inspired

- even reading dictionaries & thesauruses to make my vocabulary tighter - just so I can become a better writer.

Days & nights like this are the worse, I'm haunted by the curse of Writer's Block,

I can't seem to release because I have a Mind full of Ideas that's locked.

Individuals Divided

Now I've got a lot of thoughts & I want you all to know it,
That is my one true goal as "Demontre ThePoet".
I've got so many personalities,
but I'll share with you the 3 of them that always come to mind.
I'm so conflicted & all they do is fight for control all the time.

Now pay close attention,
because this could get confusing & I'm telling you why,
It's a story of just 3 of my many personalities
- "ME" - "MYSELF" - & "I".
"ME" loves people way too hard
& that's why people have played us,
But "MYSELF" can't get ahead in life,
because he has way too many issues with trust.

"MYSELF" always speaks his mind
& it doesn't matter if he offends others with what he has to say,
But "ME" is considered soft, because he's way too quiet
& passive most of the days.
"ME" stays calm & keeps everything mellow & mild,
While "MYSELF" is always rowdy - obnoxiously loud & wild.

"MYSELF" is bullheaded & is too stubborn to listen when others speak,
But it is "I" who is the strong one who stands tall

when the others are weak.
"I" was our strength & stayed positive when our Daddy died,
While "ME" was paralyzed in pain
& just sat down & helplessly cried.

"MYSELF" was an alcoholic
- he's selfish & doesn't know when enough is ENOUGH,
It was "I" that finally took the proper steps to finally get rid of that liquor in our cup.
"ME" never speaks up for us, so that's why we would get bullied all throughout our life,
It was "MYSELF" who didn't want to be pushed around anymore & he started to fight.

We're individuals who all know each other very well,
because our body is the same,
We express our minds differently, but our conflicts can be blamed on the same pain.
"I" tries to stop "ME" & "MYSELF" from fighting,
but they don't listen to his or my pleas,
When "I" looks into the mirror,
it's "ME" - "MYSELF" & my reflection that we all see.

We all see "I" - "MYSELF" & "ME" continue
to constantly fight for control,
This all sounds so very crazy & we now all know why,
It's so many conflicting souls together along with
"ME" - "MYSELF" & "I".

"MYSELF" - "ME" & "I" we try to be different,
but we are the same - we can't fight it,
"MYSELF" - "ME" & "I" we're all lost souls screaming loud
but our voices are still quiet.
"MYSELF" - "ME" & "I" we all try to coexist united,
"MYSELF" - "ME" & "I" all one person whose also
Individuals Divided.

Many Teardrops

I wanted her to live but she's not here,
He could've lived a great life, but he's gone,
because unknown futures cause great fear.
She could've been a loving mother & wife,
But she got taken away through an act that I considered trife.
He would've grown up to change the World,
But now he'll forever be a beautiful undiscovered Pearl.
Acts done irresponsibly most of the time have a sad result,
When things fall apart
there's usually nobody who stands up & takes the fault.
I never dreamed my name could be attached
to such a tragic event,
My time spent with he or she
would've been a time greatly spent.
The memory of what never came to be, haunts me,
A face of something precious that I will never get to see.
Anger & sorrow fills me up because it's something I can't forget,
It was not supposed to be like this & I'm full of doubts & regret.
I swear I didn't want this, but my voice went unheard,
The fact that I couldn't stop it, is honestly absurd.
A choice was made when there shouldn't have been a choice,
I'm hurt that in this situation, I didn't have a voice.

There's a spot in hell waiting for me & I do deserve it,
I should've tried harder when I prayed,

then maybe God would've heard it.

A soul's gone because I wasn't assertive,

A deceitful situation took away a life

that would've had a purpose.

I try to just move on, but I have it stuck on my mind,

If given a fair chance it could've been a joyful time.

I have a heart full of love that she won't be able to receive,

I could've shown him hope during hard times

that makes having hope hard to believe.

I have given forgiveness, though I'll always be haunted

by her hurtful act,

This is one of many reasons

I will never keep peace of mind intact.

I try not to judge her

even though this life event has left me scorned,

I'm at a loss for words for my son or daughter

- a child that was never born.

A life snatched away that never got a chance to breathe,

A life lost because it got aborted after it was conceived.

That would've been my baby boy or my girl,

but a decision was made selfishly.

It happened behind my back

& ever since my life has not been the same for me.

I tried to keep this to myself,

but my conscience wouldn't let my feelings stop,

R.I.P. to my child who never was

- you are not forgotten - your Daddy sheds many teardrops.

Your Only Son

I sit sipping my drink as I grab my pen
and my inner thoughts comes out,
I look at the stars and wonder what life is really about.
I want to change the world, but I don't have that type of clout,
I try to trust in the Lord, but I honestly do have doubts.
You took my dad and I'm still grieving,
I guess I'm still blessed because I am still breathing.
On a normal day, I have a fear to one day die,
but on days I'm feeling low, I've considered giving suicide a try.
But I can't bring more pain and tears to my mother's eyes,
plus, my kids need me here right by their side.
You've given me children that I do adore and love,
I wonder why do you just sit back
and watch us struggle from up above.
Our world is such a mess and a complete shame,
part of this is your doing - you must take some of the blame.
I hope I don't go to hell for expressing all of this,
but this is my truth and happy days from my yesterdays is something that I miss.
You're supposed to be our savior,
so I need you to please hear me,
I know your love is unconditional
and that's what we all need to see.

I keep on praying

and you haven't answered most of my prayers yet,

I think mankind's creation is something that you regret.

God, I think you've given up on your own people,

and that's the true reason

you allow, in everybody's lives, so much evil.

God, I'm saying this to you because the world needs your help,

why have you left us down here by ourselves?

God, many of us send you our pleas on blended knees,

we continue to pray, because we need your presence, PLEASE.

People keep saying you're coming back,

I'm starting to no longer believe that.

We pray to you but most times you never ever seem to come,

is it because we killed your only son?

Can't Get Things Right

Maybe it was because I didn't squash things
with my Auntie before she died,
Or it could be because I didn't see my father's pain
before he committed suicide.
Maybe because I'm a loner and I don't get out much,
or it might be because I grew up sheltered,
so when it comes to life I'm always out of touch.
It's probably because I love way too hard,
or maybe, I'm just too sensitive and take small things way too far.
It could be that I'm not close enough
to the Most High's teachings,
Or it might be that I'm not listening closely enough
when my Deacon was preaching.
It might be the fact that I have a real issue with expression,
My worst flaw is that I always keep the people I care about wondering and guessing.
It might be that my childhood is something I sorely miss,
wanting things to be like they used to be is my one true wish.
I never realized growing up
that things would so drastically change.
I often wonder how things, in my life, ended up so strange.
I honestly thought that one day I would have it all,
I simply can't remember, exactly,
when my hopes and dreams started to fall.

Life's not completely bad for me, I have many people who I consider family and they're not related by blood,
No matter how bad things get in my heart, I got nothing but love.
I know these are random thoughts,
but I hope you all still feel me,
I'm just sitting here sharing with you the real me.
Please always know that my love for everyone is forever present even when I'm away,
and it haunts me that past love shared can't always stay.
I'm always sitting at home wondering, exactly,
when did things go all wrong,
I sit there pondering while listening to old school songs.
I know I have issues because when I need to cope
I always have a cup of an 80-proof beverage in my hand.
I've lost some hope over the years,
because at times I have failed,
and failure is something I can't stand.
It's just too many times my pain is uncontainable,
It's way too many times the pain in my life has been unexplainable.
But still in all, life's a gift and I'll try to remember that,
even though I know things won't always stay intact.
I feel so empty at times,
because I can't seem to hold on to the joy
in my life with a grip that's tight,
There seems to be way too many times
that I just can't seem to get things right.

The Last Time

A tribute to my Father: Ronald O. Lewis. He passed away many years ago on May 30, 2008. Rest in Paradise. You are truly missed.

His physical presence is gone,
but those memories never go away & are here to stay,
We're all going to go one day,
but knowing when it's coming is almost impossible to say.
I miss him so much, I still can't believe his death came,
It hurts - it's an unexplainable pain.
Nobody ever knew I wanted to end it all,
and our fates could've been the same.
The hurt cripples me over & over
and it's hard to move forward
- I have a lost feeling inside that I can't explain.

We had a bond that nothing could ever break,
Why did it have to be you that death decided to take?
Your pictures bring me joy, but missing you hurts so bad,
You're the greatest role model that I could've ever had.
On the last day I saw him, we talked for hours,
It seemed just like old times, and I thought his sickness was gone
and he had regained his former power.

On the last day I saw him, he was worrying about my well-being,
so instead of saying I was fine over the phone,
I showed up in person,
so, with his own two eyes my healthy presence
he would be seeing.
On the last day I saw him, I gave him a hug,
I told him I would always be there,
and that we share a mutual love.

On the last day I saw him, I was just trying to ease his pain,
for when I was stuck in my own darkness
to help me out he did the same.
On the last day I saw him, I seen relief in his eyes,
It hurts me to admit this,
but I believe he was at peace with it being his time to die.
On the last day I saw him, he thanked me for stopping by,
I really miss my father so very much,
and as I write this, I honestly want to cry.
On the last day I saw him, it stays vividly in my mind,
because the last time I saw him
I didn't know that it would be my last time.

Never

I'm a legend that's before my time,

People feel me because they understand my grind.

I share with you thoughts that spill out of my mind,

My creativity puts together words and makes sure they rhyme.

We all have pain and I share with you mine,

My thoughts are poetic - that's why I shine.

I skillfully use metaphors to plead my case,

My words blindside you,

because they come from all over the place.

They inspire and leave you teary eyed

like you got sprayed with mace,

Plus, my phrases hit hard like trauma to the face.

I'll forever be a poetic ace,

So those who want me silenced,

I'm going to keep invading their space.

The words just pop in my head,

Then I share my thoughts so that they'll always spread.

My lyrics will last far after I am dead,

I recite them so that they are heard,

and write them down so that they are read.

Spoken word is used so people will remember what I have said,

My delivery stands strong while the weak have fled.

I surround myself with intellectuals.

Whom of which, I break bread,

It keeps my mind sharp which keeps me ahead.

I bring joy and pain because we all have had tears we've shed,
I never share the fake - I spread the real instead.
I'm a killer with expression – a poetic apocalypse,
I use vicious rhyme schemes that come from my pen
& from my lips.
I've honed my skills since I was a kid
that's how I'm able to bring you this,
My lyrics infect you like a poisonous kiss.
My words can kill or bring you bliss,
My words are highly addictive,
so, with this, I'm giving you all another fix.
I let everything out, I leave nothing in reserve,
Rhyming is my craft - just watch how I flip my words.
I've shown those who have doubted me
that a lack of faith in me is absurd,
I'm a rhyme master
that's talented in twisting all kinds of nouns and verbs.
I have no equal, I left the rest miles behind me on a vacant curb,
If rhyming was a race, I would be 1st and 2nd,
my closest competition wouldn't even finish third!!!!
The way I use wordplay is very clever,
It even surprises me how I put my rhymes together.
The way my lyrics flow is unbelievable
they can't be matched, not ever.

It's scary how flawlessly I use them
to describe my many life endeavors.
My skills are angelic and delicate like a feather,
But they're also an unstoppable force like a flood
or any other destructive type of weather.
My rhyme slanging is going to last forever,
So if you question when I'm going to stop
– the answer to that is…….. NEVER.

My parents, Ronald and Margaret Lewis

www.ingramcontent.com/pod-product-compliance
Lightning Source LLC
Chambersburg PA
CBHW071212160426
43196CB00011B/2270